The Man Who
Talks to Dogs

The Man Who Talks to Dogs

The Story of America's Wild Street Dogs

and Their Unlikely Savior

Thomas Dunne Books

St. Martin's Press ≈ New York

Melinda Roth

Preface by Tony La Russa
Foreword by Dr. Michael W. Fox

THOMAS DUNNE BOOKS.
An imprint of St. Martin's Press.

www.stmartins.com

Photographs by James Bielmann and Melinda Roth

Book design and title page photograph by James Sinclair

ISBN 0-312-28397-0

10   9   8   7   6   5

In memory of Ellie

Contents

Acknowledgments

Thanks to Alicia, Jacob, Sarah, Adam, Amelia Wolf, Susan Jackson, and Nicolyn and George Rau for their love, PJ Grim for all of her support, Paul Humbert for his patience, Dr. Ed Migneco for always being there, Julie Castiglia for her help, Sally Kim, editor at Thomas Dunne Books, for her ability to see beyond the words, and the Stray Rescue Family in St. Louis.

The first Noel . . . It was the first time Randy heard the unspoken plea "Don't leave me here." It was like my experience on the field of the Oakland A's over ten years ago, when Evie, a stray cat, ran onto the field because it was her only home: Randy Grim became impassioned about saving stray animals after his first encounter with Noel on the wintry streets of St. Louis.

In my book, Randy (whom one character calls "the Coyote Man"), Dr. Ed, and fellow volunteers Peggy and Ellie are the true heroes of St. Louis. Their patience and caring for fellow city-dwellers like Bonnie, Sunshine, Compton, Sunny, Taz, and Katlin (just a few of the friends you'll meet in this book) are unswerving. They didn't start out to build the Stray Rescue of St. Louis organization, but with the support of a community that appreciated their service and the enormity of their goal to respond to every "Don't leave me here" look, the organization was born and thrives today.

I have long believed in the special connection between animals and people. Randy's own story of being saved by the dogs of our city is a great illustration of the power animals have to give us strength and add value to our lives.

As you'll learn from the humane education that fills many of the chapters of this book, over 6 million animals are euthanized in America's animal shelters every year. What Randy and his compatriots know is that for every one of those animals, several more, maybe dozens, live on the streets of our cities and towns.

In the pages that follow, you'll find a blend of tales and animal facts that would be a great component of any humane education program. If I could make it happen, I would make Randy's story required reading in all middle schools.

I know you'll enjoy reading about Randy and his friends. I hope you'll finish the book with a greater understanding and courage to see the look in the eyes of unwanted animals that seem to say "Don't leave me here."

Tony La Russa
Founder of the Animal Rescue Foundation
Manager of the St. Louis Cardinals

This book is an inspiration for all those people whose love and concern for dogs and all creatures will move them to go where even angels might fear to tread.

Most people have never seen the underbelly of America and few have gone to the places where lost, abandoned, and feral dogs, sometimes in packs, roam the wastelands of urban ghettoes, abandoned communities, and decaying blocks of warehouses and factories.

Almost thirty years ago, I studied one such pack in a rundown part of St. Louis, Missouri, which moved me to write about their plight, and which also prepared me for dog rescue work in the Third World, currently in India. The United States is the only non-Third-World country that has this problem to the degree demonstrated in this book. It is no overstatement to say that the problem of homeless dogs in America and their suffering, so vividly documented in this book—compounded by the suffering of those dogs who are trained by depraved people to fight and kill other dogs—is a plight shared by hundreds of millions of homeless dogs around the world in less developed countries.

What happens to a person whose caring, even broken, heart is touched and opened by the plight of a fellow creature, and whose spirit is called to action, like the man in this book, whose calling it is to rescue homeless dogs? Read this book and meet one of my heroes, Randy Grim.

What happens when "man's best friend," the dog, becomes one of the unseen victims of urban decay, poverty, and crime that spreads like cancer into the heart of society? Most homeless dogs are lost souls, disoriented and condemned to the abyss between the wild and the tame. They are tormented by the incomprehensible nature of their condition, neither belonging nor free, unless and until they can find a pack and can recall the ancient rituals and codes of conduct for cooperation and survival. Survival for how long in an environment in which they do not belong and did not deserve to suffer? Until they die, or are rescued and rehabilitated, rather than being exterminated by various lethal and often cruel means for reasons of public health and safety. Mass extermination is no solution, since killing only makes room for more to fill the abyss. Read this book and rage and cry with me.

Why are so many powerful breeds, like the Rottweiler, American Pit Bull, Chow Chow, and mixed breeds thereof, running wild, diseased, and starving in urban wastelands? Why are they and other smaller breeds and mixes often found severely injured, tortured, dying or dead, thrown into Dumpsters and tossed onto vacant lots? Read this book and be inspired by the passion of dog rescuer Randy Grim, and other kindred spirits like Dr. Edward Migneco, who share his pain and love and dedication.

Thanks to author and investigative reporter Melinda Roth, whose empathy, wit and wisdom, deep understanding of the emotional suffering of homeless dogs, as well as her sympathetic resonance with Randy, result in a captivating narrative. She also provides a well-researched and documented review of dog behavior, communication, and psychology, and also of urban dog problems, "puppy mill" breeders, and dog fighters.

Read this book and "GET A LIFE," as Randy would say. Rescue a dog; adopt or foster a homeless dog; support those committed and courageous souls who have abandoned a "normal" life for a life of service through compassionate action; volunteer at your local animal shelter and help raise funds for adoption, law enforcement, cruelty investigations, spay and neuter, and humane education programs.

This book is a clarion call for civic action in all communities at home and abroad for dogs' sake. The health and well-being of dogs and other animals, wild and domestic, are clear indicators of the health and well-being of every human community and of our moral progress as a humane and responsible species.

Dr. Michael W. Fox
Veterinarian, bioethicist, and author

No one has any idea how many wild dogs live on America's city streets. Probably not too many people care. I didn't when I first interviewed Randy Grim in 1999 for a story that appeared in the St. Louis *Riverfront Times,* when I drove around with him for weeks in an unheated twenty-one-year-old VW bus through neighborhoods as ravaged as Third World countries, chasing dogs that were like creatures from another planet.

I'd just returned from three years as a political correspondent in the state capital and I wasn't used to these sorts of urban safaris. Besides, politics is as hard to clean from your system as cholesterol, so as Randy drove through poor neighborhoods and explained his mission of rescuing wild dogs, my mind drifted to the social and political deficit around us, to the bombed-out houses, fields of trash, secondary forests where schools and churches used to be.

East St. Louis, for example, was once a thriving river town, but now half of the city's residents survive on public assistance and 20 percent live on less than $5,000 annually. Because the city budget couldn't support garbage pickup for several years and even now removal is sporadic, residents must either burn trash in their yards or dump it in the ever-growing number of empty lots and empty buildings. As the piles of ash and garbage bags rise higher, nature reclaims lost territory and provides lush cover and scrounging grounds for animals. Snakes, frogs, and turtles thrive in abandoned stockyard swamps. Coyotes and deer haunt the edges of town. Once, as we chased an elusive Pit Bull through a decaying residential neighborhood, Randy slammed on the brakes to let a family of quail cross the street.

One day, with the human tragedy spilling out onto the streets of East St. Louis before us, I finally blurted the question that had badgered my conscience from the start of our interviews: "Don't you think your time and energy would be better spent helping people?"

Randy just shrugged.

"Look around you," I persisted. "I mean, they're just *dogs.*"

He shrugged again.

"It's a really hard thing to explain," he said.

His personality certainly didn't give up any clues, and I was mystified by his devotion. He was a well-educated, successful, thirty-five-year-old business owner who was sardonic, easily stressed, and disillusioned with the human race. He didn't like children and he made fun of old people. His laundry list of phobias included drinking tap water, walking through grocery stores, and driving on highways. He smoked too much and suffered incapacitating panic attacks. Yet as founder of Stray Rescue of St. Louis, he spent his days chasing wild, injured, diseased dogs that no one else would touch.

In my research for the newspaper story, I learned that more than 62 million dogs are kept as pets in this country, and that three out of every five American households include a dog or cat. Of the individuals who have a pet, 48 percent consider themselves emotionally dependent on the animal, and another 27 percent spend more time with their dogs and cats than with friends or family.

But America's obsession with its pets has a dark side. The number of stray and feral dogs is increasing at rates that alarm both health officials and animal-control experts across the country. As many as 10 million dogs and cats are euthanized in pounds and shelters every single year, and for every one of those, countless more live on the streets. An increasing number are feral, which means they descend from domesticated dogs but are born in the wild, grow up on the streets, and won't come near humans no matter how hungry they are. Relatively little is known about their actual numbers; less still about how they survive.

The problem is most acute in poor neighborhoods where people buy dogs for protection and sport fighting but can't afford to feed them, let alone get them spayed or neutered. As the unsterilized dogs roam free, the abandoned buildings and industrial wastelands allow them safe places to congregate.

During our rides and interviews, Randy and I found a lot of dead dogs, some shot, some hit by cars, some just curled up in the warmest place they could find before they fell asleep and died. Not much better off were the ones who still lived—skittish and skeletal and missing ears and tails—some bald from mange, others in skins of scabs. Randy was driving around in a Teutonic tin can, spending thousands of his own dollars to pay for their vet bills and thousands of hours more to heal their emotional scars. The dying dogs haunted me, too, but this man devoted every physical and mental resource to helping them.

"I just don't get it," I said.

"It's a hard thing to explain. It's like . . . when I'm out here driving around . . . you know, and . . . and . . . I see them, and they look up at me . . . you know . . . I can hear them . . . hear them talking to me."

"Oh?"

Randy nodded.

"And what do they have to say, exactly?"

"It's a really hard thing to explain."

"Let me guess. 'Where have all the Milk Bones gone?' 'See Randy run?' I know, I know—'Who let the dogs—' "

Randy, always in the shadow of overwhelming frustration because he felt no one around him understood, banged his palms on the steering wheel and turned his face toward the side window.

"No."

Then, deflated, he let his shoulders relax, and his hands slid to the bottom of the wheel.

"They say . . . 'Don't *leave* me here.' "

After the newspaper story was published, Randy and I became friends, even though hanging around with him meant finding, feeding, and chasing wild dogs. It meant traipsing through abandoned buildings, running down highways, climbing over barbed-wire fences, and crawling through weeds.

Several months into our new friendship, Randy, his domestic partner, Paul Humbert, and I went camping in Memphis, near Graceland; we woke up the first morning in the campground to find two male dogs, one female, and her eight-week-old puppy scrounging through our garbage. A homeless veteran who lived in the park told us that the pack usually stayed in the woods, coming out at dawn and dusk to clean up scraps at the campsites.

As we watched them cling to the edges of the woods, Randy named the Coonhound Elvis, the black Lab Peabody, the chocolate-brown Lab mix Belle, and her black puppy Prissy. Because Randy didn't have equipment to trap the dogs, he gave the veteran some dog food and $20 and asked him to feed the pack until we came back the following weekend.

On the way home, my first question to Randy was " 'We'?" I had no interest in traveling all the way back from St. Louis to Memphis, through five hours of southern Missouri and the flattest part of Arkansas, to trap three mangy dogs and a wild puppy. But all through the next week, I found myself thinking about Belle, and about how she had probably delivered a full litter of puppies out there, alone in the woods, and then defended them and fed them and kept them dry when it rained only to watch them die anyway, one by one.

The next weekend, *we* drove back to Memphis. With the help of the homeless man and a group of Harley-Davidson riders who had stopped at the park for the night, we trapped the three adults— Elvis, Peabody, and Belle. But Prissy hid well in the woods, and by late Sunday night, with the realities of Monday staring us hard in the face, we realized she had to stay behind.

She was weaned, so we gave the homeless man another $20, some dog food, and a trap, even though his chances of catching her were slim. As we pulled away, I looked back and saw the tiny wild thing hovering alone at the edge of the woods. It was probably the first time she'd been alone in her life.

For the next five days, Elvis, Peabody, and Belle stayed at the vet clinic in St. Louis. I visited daily, and as I watched Belle through the kennel door one afternoon—thin, shivering, pathetic, and alone—I heard myself tell her, this dog, that I'd go back for her puppy. I promised her, out loud.

By Friday, however, Randy came down with the flu, so I bribed my son, Jacob, to go with me back to Memphis, and we drove back through five hours of southern Missouri and the flattest part of Arkansas for Prissy. Who was in the trap when we got there. Who bit maniacally at Jacob when he pulled her out. Who defecated all over the car on the way home. Who greeted Belle with yips and leaps of joy when she saw her. Who, one week later, was in a loving foster home and was as tame as if she'd been born on a blanket on a bed, instead of on the cold, wet ground of the woods.

Elvis, the Coonhound, recovered from his mange and went to a permanent home as well. Soon after, his new parents sent Randy a photograph of him sitting *on* their kitchen table. Peabody was adopted by one of the vet technicians at the clinic and also learned to adjust to living in a human pack.

As for Belle, she lives with me now.

I guess I heard something. I heard it when we drove away from the campground that Sunday night, when the three adult dogs were in the bus and on their way to safety, and I looked back and saw Prissy, there at the edge of the dark woods, small and all alone.

Don't leave me here.

It's a really hard thing to explain.

Part One

Chapter One

The First: Noel

The blizzard barreled down on the dark city at fifty miles per hour, and as the wind whipped power lines in the air like jump ropes and sent empty shopping carts racing with loose debris down the curb, ice pellets slammed up against the side of the ancient, unheated lime-green Volkswagen bus that crawled down Chouteau Street doing ten.

Inside the bus, Randy Grim gripped the steering wheel and repeated after the voice on his stress-management tape:

"FEAR IS INSTINCTUAL."

"Fear is instinctual."

"FEAR IS AN ILLUSION."

"Fear is an illusion."

"YOU CHOOSE TO BE AFRAID."

Cold air blew from the heater and the ailing muffler rattled windows dotted with *South Park* decals. Coffee spilled from foam cup; the floor was already littered with wet snow, old blankets, Sonic Burger wrappers, and dog-food cans that rolled from one end of the bus to the other. On the dashboard, above an overflowing ashtray, was a manufacturer's warning: *"Fahren nur mit verriegeltem Dach!"*

Outside, snow blew in horizontal sheets across railroad yards, fields littered with twisted metal, and abandoned factories that stood like tombstones in a cemetery no one tended anymore. Across the road, redbrick row houses stared back in graffiti-gilded defeat. Uninhabited, lit only by the glow of downtown St. Louis six blocks north, the street seemed in no need of basic electricity anymore.

"FEAR CREATES STRESS."

"Fear creates stress."

"STRESS CREATES FEAR."

"Stress creates fear."

"YOU CHOOSE TO BE AFRAID."

Randy's boot stayed on the brake pedal. Windshield wipers slapped across glass. In the beam of his one working headlight, eyelets of cobblestones filled up with snow. Ice set like varnish on everything else.

"I choose to be afraid. I choose to be afraid. I choose to be afraid."

A wind gust toyed with the balance of the bus. Randy yanked a cigarette out of his coat pocket.

"I *choose* to be afraid. . . ."

If the tread on the tires had been any thicker, he would have hit the thin yellow dog who shot from the black of the warehouse yard and into the band of headlights on the road, streaking from one edge of night to the other. Instead, Randy jammed his boot on the brake. A bald-tire slide. A skate across the ice. The steering wheel spun through his fingers as the bus pirouetted toward the curb, sending blankets, muddy gloves, and dog-food cans flying like clothes spinning round in a dryer.

"Whoooa!"

The bus bounced off the edge of the curb, spun, and hit the curb again. Then, as if in slow motion, the front end of the bus sailed up—"Whoooa!"—and crashed back down to earth.

Randy stared out the side of a redbrick building. By his one headlight he could read the baroque graffiti: "Plur" . . . "FanDang" . . . "Gooze Boy."

"FEAR IS AN IRRATIONAL EMOTION."

He swiveled and looked out the side window to the street, where the yellow dog had vanished in a cyclone of white. Without turning off the engine, he reached behind the front seat and grabbed a black leather snare, pushed open the door, and jumped from the bus. His boots slid out from under him and he fell to the ground on his knees. He climbed up along the open door, dodging stabs of snow and ice, feeling his way blind along the side of the bus until he plunged out onto the street.

The chase was made as much on hands and knees as on foot, bolting forward, falling, gaining his balance, clutching at outcroppings of ice, falling again. It was like dancing on sheets of grease.

Ten yards ahead, the yellow dog ran up the middle of the road. Randy followed after her through a field of drifting snow. Then behind a line of darkened row houses. Then up a flight of stairs. Then across the top landing.

With no place left to go, the yellow dog turned, faced Randy, backed into a corner, and pinned her large ears back as she bared her teeth in silence. She was a small-boned German Shepherd mix with ribs jutting from her body like a splayed fan, and her eyes darted from Randy to the snare in his hand to the ground two stories below. The wind blew snow onto her face.

"Don't j-j-j-ump." The cold minced the words between his teeth. "I-I-I-t's okay. I-I-I-t's okay. I prom-m-m-ise, girl, tr-r-r-ust me."

He went down on one knee and put the snare on the porch and

held his hand out toward the dog nose. Her top lip curled up to show more teeth, but her head turned sideways, into the wind, because she didn't want to see what scared her.

"Don't be a-f-f-f-raid. Tr-r-r-ust me."

The wind clamored across the landing as if dragging chains behind it, and as Randy wrapped his fingers around the snare and slid his knees forward along the porch, the dog looked down to the ground, where wind sucked up snow eddies and flung them out into the night.

"It's g-g-g-oing t-t-t-o be okay."

Cold tremors raced through his arms, which felt lawless and distant and asleep. Like something he didn't own. He moved the snare toward the dog's head, and she flattened her body against the wall as her front legs curled up into her chest.

"P-p-p-lease don't be scared."

Behind Randy, a screen door slapped against brick. The dog's eyes shot over Randy's shoulder, and he spun on his knees.

"Don't move."

An old woman stood in the darkened doorway with her arms stretched forward, as if dowsing for water. Randy stared up the nostrils of a small black gun and shoved his hands up toward the sky.

"I *said*, don't move."

"I'm t-t-t-ry-ing to g-g-g-et the, the, the d-d-d-og."

The woman waved the gun toward the stairs.

"Get your mongrel off my property, or I'll shoot you both."

"She's n-n-n-ot my d-d-d-og."

"Now!"

Randy spun back toward the dog and swung the snare like a lasso toward her neck. It landed true, but when he drew it in, the yellow dog reared up on her back legs and twisted left then right, away from the pull of the noose. Randy vaulted forward and grabbed her around the midsection, but she yelped and bit at his shoulder.

"You gonna git off my property or not?"

The woman, her robe flapping against her legs, wagged the pistol back and forth between the stairs and Randy. He grabbed the dog again and pulled her backward down the stairs with her heart pounding in his palms.

He reached the ground and stumbled across the yard, the old woman's threats still following him in muffled rounds through the wind: ". . . not afraid of you . . . mean it . . . my property . . . mine . . ."

Out on the sidewalk half a block away, the bus rattled on the curb with its headlight splashed up against the brick wall. Randy dropped the dog to the ground. She thrashed and twisted against the snare like a bass against a hook; his numb fingers couldn't hold the snare against her bucks and twirls, so he shifted the handle to the heels of his clenched palms and pulled her backward toward the bus.

"Come on, girl. You can do it. You can do it."

The dog, terrified, collapsed into instinct and feigned lifelessness.

"Please, please get up."

Randy tightened the snare between his palms, but the dog's fear weighed her down. He couldn't pull her anymore, and because she was uphill from him on the plane of ice, he couldn't get the footing to step forward and grab her.

He shifted the snare's handle up under his armpit and turned toward the bus. But as he moved head down into the wind, his boots lost their grip, and he floundered to the ground and felt the snare rip away. He grabbed for it wildly, uselessly; he couldn't lose her now, and as he watched the snare's black handle slip away like a snake through the snow, the little yellow dog followed the momentum of his own fall and slid forward on the ice and into his arms.

Back inside the bus, Randy held his hands in front of heater vents that wheezed cold air.

"YOU ARE GIVING TOO MUCH FROM YOUR OWN BASKET."

Randy punched the eject button on the tape player and looked back at the dog, who was shivering on a pile of blankets.

"Your name is Noel, okay? Everything is going to be fine. I promise."

But cold and fear rippled through her skeletal body, and she turned her head away and stared at the side of the bus.

"I know how scared you are. But your bad days are all behind you now. Trust me."

Ice ticked on the roof and against the windshield and glistened in the shaft of his headlights. He yanked the bus into reverse, and as it clanked back up and over the curb and he pulled out onto the street, he glanced toward the abandoned warehouse where snow rolled like tumbleweed across its black yard.

He stepped on the brake.

While he could barely make out the hulking silhouette of the building through the sheets of the storm, the shapes in its yard were unmistakable.

"Oh, no."

Shadows in a line. Skeletal in the snow.

It was a pack.

Noel's pack.

And like ghostly lawn ornaments in the night, they sat in the yard, and they watched him.

Chapter Two

On the Street

One Year Later

The bus rumbled north from East St. Louis toward Washington Park, lunging in and out of potholes the size of small craters. The sky was low, the streets were wet, and the forecast called for snow. As he drove past abandoned gas stations, peeling billboards, and all-night drive-through liquor shops, Randy lit another cigarette and steered clear of dead dogs in the road.

In the tape deck, Gregorian chants set to an electronic dance beat thumped like an ancient running commentary on the Apocalypse to come. The bus passed iron-barred pawnshops and bombed-out cars and burned-down houses filled with garbage and snow. It passed topless bars with hand-painted signs, passed coatless men babbling up to the sky.

"These are prime areas." Randy pointed through the crack that was gaining ground across his soot-spattered windshield. "Wherever there are empty buildings, abandoned homes, junkyards, that's where you find them."

Randy edged the bus into an intersection with flashing yellow streetlights, then froze at the wheel: a brown Buick swerved around him with a violent rush of air. The streetlights, like garbage collection and police protection, worked only sporadically on the East Side, when the city council found the funds, so one's success in traversing these steel-and-concrete barrens depended on luck and fairly good timing. The quality of life here ran on much the same.

The bus drove on. Past barbershops in jerry-built shacks and roofless schools with trees growing inside. Past fields of rusted refrigerators, old boats, wood pallets, and shot-out televisions by the dozen. In the previous two decades, the city's manufacturing base had dropped by one-third, the wholesale trade by nearly two-thirds, and the retail trade by yet more than that; the number of crimes committed annually exceeded the number of people who still lived here, and the average annual income was less than the price of a decent used car. Randy seemed oblivious to the social wreckage around him.

He was looking for dogs.

And as he drove past long-defunct banks strangled by frozen brown vines and housing projects infiltrated by brush, Randy scanned the wreckage as if window shopping.

At Pennsylvania and Fourth Streets, a Pit Bull and a large Shepherd mix scrounged through the remains of a grade school Dumpster. Two blocks south, several other dogs trotted up the train tracks and followed them north. At the next corner, a large black Chow stood guard on a hill, while an unclassifiable victim of advanced mange hobbled on three balding legs down the middle of the street.

These were among the city's wild dogs, those the pounds can't catch and the humane shelters won't deal with. Dogs like them colonize whatever neighborhoods afford them the best shelter, the most food, and the least contact with human beings, where they can exist like genetic castaways on the third rail between domesticity and wildness.

The truly feral dogs are born on the streets and are as wild as wolves in the woods. Only they aren't wolves; while some instinct still hovers at the edges of their awareness, they are the end product of thousands of years of domestication. Their wild ancestors would have organized themselves in packs under highly structured parameters for protection, reproduction, and hunting, but now they are evolutionary misfits who don't have a clue.

At dawn and at dusk they come out from hiding to travel the alleys, roam the parks, congregate in and around empty buildings to hunt, scrounge, or steal anything to eat, anything at all. Their poverty hinges on that of humans, so wherever there are dilapidated structures, trash-strewn culverts, or open fields of rusting junk, there are wild dogs. Trailer courts, scrap yards, housing projects: inside every boarded-up church are the bodies of dead dogs; behind every wall of graffiti, a newborn litter of feral pups.

Randy ejected the techno-Gregorian chants from the tape deck and pushed in Tears for Fears: "Welcome to your life. There's no turning back . . ."

"It's my rescue music," he said.

As the bus rattled cast on Monk Street, two young dogs watched it roll by from a forest of cottonwood trees and telephone poles that stood connected to nothing. In this part of town there were more empty houses than occupied ones, more feral dogs than automobiles. Bombs dropped on a neighborhood would have caused less ruin.

"There are thousands of them in this area alone," Randy said as he flicked his cigarette out the window. "But you know, your average tax accountant doesn't usually drive to these kinds of places to take the kids out for ice cream. You know what I mean? So they don't see this."

As founder of Stray Rescue—a position roughly equivalent, he said, to being captain of a punctured life raft—Randy makes this trek through the East Side regularly, sometimes to feed an established pack, sometimes to track down a new one, today to search for a large group recently sighted moving in and out of an empty house.

Randy jabbed his finger at the windshield. Two yellow dogs raced along a distant chain-link fence that separated I-64 from the town. They were thin, matted, and running hard. Probably second- or third-generation street dogs, he said, who wouldn't come near humans and were unlikely to live past their second year. "Gunshot wounds, starvation, slit throats, heartworm"; Randy ticked off the assassins in staccato.

At the next intersection, a large black Shepherd mix lay dead on the pavement. Farther on, two puppies ran for cover in an abandoned field, and another Shepherd mix, probably their mother, lay dead near a trash-strewn curb. At the next street, a pack of ten dogs pursued a female in heat; but congregations of twenty or more weren't uncommon this time of year.

"They're basically just like two-year-old children out here," he said. "I mean, they try to form packs and live by wolf rules, only they don't really know what the rules are. . . . It's like they're trying to *play* wild, only they don't know how. They might as well be living on the moon."

A hole in the muffler competed with the music for attention, and as Randy turned up the volume on the tape deck, the bus bounced through a pothole and sent canceled checks, wet receipts, and crumpled cigarette packs dancing across the dashboard. Outside, black slush spanked the sides of the van as broken glass and gravel played a game of hit-and-run. The wind picked up, and as Randy steered the bus through the streets, children on their way to school pointed and laughed at the braying pontoon boat in the road until blasts from the tailpipe sent them running for cover.

Randy could have afforded a better vehicle. He owned a trendy dog-grooming shop where he charged as much for an oatmeal bath and butt trim as residents in the city's housing projects spent on a week's worth of groceries. His income neared six digits, and he spent most of the money on the dogs.

"It's, you know, hard for me to explain why I do what I do," he said. "My friends, what's left of them anyway, sit me down and talk to me like I'm an alcoholic, you know, in hushed voices, with looks of deep concern.

"Paul tells me to my face that he thinks I'm crazy, but we've been together for almost twelve years now, and I've learned that the secret is to make him feel like it's all his fault somehow. He's a flight attendant, so he's away a lot, and I use that as the excuse."

An Akita mix trotted across a side street. A thin brindle Pit Bull scurried into a field. On the side of Monk Street, swaddled in a frozen, gray sheet, lay a dead German Shepherd with ice on its fur.

"My mom blames herself."

Randy spotted the house he was looking for, a white-frame cadaver. In the mud of what was once its front yard, an aging man and woman combed through a pile of beer bottles, broken baby furniture, family photographs, mattress springs, molding clothes, and plastic garbage bags long emptied of edible scraps. Randy pulled the bus to the curb.

"Look at that." He pointed beyond the couple in the yard to a woolly red Chow on the front porch of the house.

The little red lion stared back at the van. A large brown-and-white Husky stalked past him into the house.

Randy cut the engine. Besides a strengthening north wind and the distant, muffled sound of traffic on the interstate, the only sound was the flapping of a curtain through jagged glass in a front window.

The lion on the porch didn't move, just concentrated on the van with aggressive aloofness; the lumbering shadows of other large dogs searched for cover in the darkness behind him.

Randy rarely hunted neutered Poodles or Schnauzers. From the economic vantage point of a low-income resident in a high-crime neighborhood, the most affordable burglar alarm is a feisty Pit Bull or Mastiff, and the feistiest Pit Bull or Mastiff is the one who isn't sterilized. And because unaltered dogs tend to roam and pack up, and because animal control wardens are as scarce as veterinarians (neither exists in East St. Louis or Washington Park), Pit Bulls, Rottweilers, German Shepherds, and Mastiffs breed, run, fight, and mate in small packs on the streets.

Randy reached into his coat pocket pulled out a crumpled pack of cigarettes. He looked, as if for the first time, at the old couple working their way through the garbage in the yard.

"People always ask me why I don't care more about people," he said as smoke twirled around his head in thick rings. "Frankly, I'm really sick of that question."

He sized up the situation in the house and shook his head. He shouldn't be out here today. He couldn't take in any more dogs. He had dogs at the vet's, dogs doubled up in foster homes, dogs in his mother's garage. He'd already called in every favor he could think of, real or made up, and his network of friends, volunteers, and sympathetic family members was stressed to the point of fracture.

Besides, the dogs in the house were strong. They had shelter. They weren't starving. Today alone he'd seen a dozen others who wouldn't make it through the coming storm.

But even that wasn't the real reason he wouldn't catch the dogs in the house. The real reason lay folded in a small paper bag tacked unabashedly to the house's front door frame. Behind the Chow who still hadn't moved. Who wouldn't move except to attack. To attack as specifically trained.

Randy flicked his cigarette out the window.

"It's a crack house," he said, and shoved the bus into reverse.

No organizations keep tabs on feral and stray dogs in America. "There are no actual numbers," says Dr. Stephen Zawistowski, senior vice president of animal sciences and science adviser for the American Society for the Prevention of Cruelty to Animals (ASPCA) in New York City. "There just isn't enough data. We've invested almost no research money (as a country) in stray dogs. It's much easier to get funding for the research of, say, mountain lions, because there's almost a prejudice in the science community that domestic animals aren't 'worthy.' "

Some experts estimate the stray population by counting the numbers of dogs euthanized by shelters every year—anywhere between 5 million and 9 million, according to the Humane Society of the United States—and then guessing that for each one of those, several more, maybe dozens more, still live out on the streets. Others, like Alan M. Beck of the Center for the Human-Animal Bond at Purdue University, point out that animal-shelter data is really only an estimate of owned-dog populations, not stray populations.

It's an underground epidemic, relegated for the most part to uninhabited and poverty-stricken urban terrain where, since the 1980s, increased crime has led to an increase in ownership of large dogs of breeds perceived as protective. But because of several generations of breeding for aggressiveness combined with declining animal control resources, fewer and fewer urban veterinarians, and an increase in organized dogfighting, there are more and more unneutered and unspayed Pit Bulls, Rottweilers, Chows, and German Shepherds living on the streets and producing feral offspring.

"I suspect it's an increasing problem in communities in flux," Zawistowski says. "In areas where there is urban decay, you've got the folks who want large, aggressive dogs because they're a status symbol, and the other group of folks want them for protection. If they become disenchanted with the dog or they can't afford to take care of them, the dogs form groups to find food and shelter."

In Detroit, the third most common complaint lodged at City Hall in 1998–99 was that packs of wild dogs roamed the city streets. Postal carriers stopped delivering mail in some areas because of the threat posed by dangerous strays. According to news reports, people in some Detroit neighborhoods were routinely trapped in their homes because of aggressive stray dogs; at the time this book was written, the situation was unchanged.

In New Orleans, an estimated 40,000 or more stray dogs walk the streets at night and disappear at dawn, while in San Diego, large, elusive packs of dogs live along the banks of the San Luis Rey River. Jacksonville, Chicago, Los Angeles, and Dallas each report more than 25,000 stray dogs picked up by animal control wardens annually, and in Salt Lake City, packs of large dogs use "hyenalike" tactics to get food, according to Salt Lake County Animal Services workers.

During the 1990s, packs of dogs have colonized urban zoos, including the Cleveland Metropark Zoo, the St. Louis Zoo, and the Bronx Zoo, where zoo officials, who were within their legal rights to protect the other animals, shot them.

In the past ten years, New York City, Cleveland, Baltimore, Houston, Indianapolis, Santa Fe, Pittsburgh, Washington, D.C., and Miami have all reported an epidemic of stray and feral dogs.

In Los Angeles, an estimated 50,000 stray dogs prowl through the city and county on any given night, and the packs of Pit Bulls and Rottweilers used to guard crack houses have been designated by local police as "the latest gangs." In 1999, SWAT teams of police, sheriff's deputies, and animal control officers went out on daily sweeps of the city and county where 200,000 residents were bitten, and at least forty-seven vicious stray dogs—of the hundreds caught every day—had to be shot in one year. In some neighborhoods, residents carried rocks to scare off the dogs.

In the month of February 2000, more than 2,000 dogs passed through the doors of the South-Side Animal Shelter, operated by Los Angeles County Animal Care and Control, but because there were only fifty-four holding pens, more than eighty dogs were euthanized every day just to make room for more.

Says Madeline Bernstein, president of the Los Angeles SPCA: "You've got a situation where people complain that there are too many dogs out there, and the department complains that they don't have enough money to pick them up, and meanwhile the number of dogs multiplies, and it just goes on and on."

Sleet spilled from a steel-plated sky, and with the temperature losing its grip on 30 degrees, the wind would soon freeze dry tree limbs, car antennas, and power lines. The bus drove on. Past sidewalks upended by tree roots. Walls of old churches that fenced in young forests. Hollowed-out Laundromats filled in with snow. Gray empty rail yards circled by hawks. Past dogs. Loose dogs, chained dogs, dead dogs in the road.

Past a small black Chow shivering next to the ruins of a burned-out house. Randy pumped the brakes.

"I never leave here without taking one of them back with me."

He pulled the bus up and let it idle as the Chow lifted his head from his outstretched front legs. Ice pellets lodged in his fur, but he panted heavily, as if suffering from heatstroke, and when Randy turned off the bus's engine, the Chow dropped his head back down onto his paws.

"He's dying."

Heartworm, Randy guessed, had slowly drained the Chow's desire to do anything but sleep. Even during an ice storm. Eventually, if he didn't freeze to death first, the Chow's heart would fail, and the separation from life would come as quietly as a long cold trip into a bottomless dream.

Randy stared out the front window as ice hit the roof in rapid ticks.

"I'm afraid of things, you know." He winced, as if the sudden confession were something being shoved into a sunlit yard after years in solitary confinement. He stared out the window and then laughed.

"Lots of things. Everything, really." He lit a cigarette. "Public places, fluorescent lights, parties, elevators, driving. Technically, I have panic attacks, but I prefer to think of them as issues."

He popped two rings of smoke from his mouth. "Germs, they're a *real* big issue. I disinfect everything and never, ever eat at buffets. I can't put my hands on escalator railings—if, that is, I can get myself on the escalator in the first place—and public bathrooms, forget it. I mean, thank God there's a cure for leprosy. I have to take one Xanax for driving, one and a half for shopping malls, two for walking through an airport, and three if I have to *eat* in an airport."

His laugh was forced from some low place in his throat. "But being out here, I'm not afraid of anything, you know?

"I have my groceries delivered, because I get panicky in grocery stores, but if there's wild dog, and I have to get groovy canned cat food in order to catch him, then I'll run into any store and buy it. Just like that. I don't even think about it. And, like, I usually drive ten miles out of my way on back streets to avoid driving on a highway—I *hate* driving on highways—but if there's an emergency with a dog somewhere, I don't even think about anything except getting there as fast as I can.

"It's like rescuing the dogs makes me face my phobias, but that's really hard to explain to people. My therapist is totally confused."

He refocused on the Chow. "His hair isn't matted, and his nails aren't worn down, so he probably isn't feral. That's one good thing, anyway."

The door hinges screamed as Randy eased out of the bus. When he lowered himself onto the pavement, the Chow's head came up again. He was small, and his black eyes, two listless voids, peered out from under black hair.

"Hey there," Randy said.

Because he understood the dog's fear like his own, he understood the value of a low, innocuous approach and hunched down to make his advance less threatening. In one gloved hand he held a glob of cat food, in the other the long black snare.

Chows are unpredictable. On the surface, they seem reserved, but there is often a well-organized offensive lining up behind their cool stares. When most dogs feel threatened, they broadcast their fear with raised tails, ears, and shackles, but most Chows size things up internally, analytically, conclusively, then attack without any warning.

"I understand, little guy. I understand."

The trick was to display as much calming authority as he could. This was a dog bred to guard, to disconnect sense from sentimentality, so unless an unruly dominance flowed through his character, he wouldn't turn aggressive if he didn't see the need. And if the Chow was as physically weak as he seemed, and if Randy made clear his neutral intentions, the dog would surrender.

"You want to come home with me, huh?"

Randy moved his eyes from the Chow's front paws up to his glassy, watchful eyes, then back down to his paws. As he inched closer, the Chow stood up and backed away.

"You don't have to be afraid."

Randy held the food out toward the Chow, but physical weakness confused the dog, mixed up the wiring in his judgment so that fear, anger, and a need to belong yanked at him from all directions.

"Trust me, I understand."

The Chow whimpered, sat down, then thumped his tail warily on the ground to let Randy know that he didn't really care where on this two-rung hierarchy he stood, just wanted to know where he stood for sure. Randy dropped the snare to the ground. The Chow opened his mouth in a wide, subordinate grin, which meant the mental tug-of-war was over.

"You're a brave dog."

The Chow shuffled toward Randy's outstretched hand. Since he wasn't feral, he would be much easier to place in a foster home than a wild dog. But Randy believes that every one of them, no matter how unsocialized or aggressive or physically challenged, can be reintroduced into the human pack in time.

The problem now was the Chow's health. If he had heartworm, as Randy suspected from his lethargy, cough, and thinness, the treatment would be expensive. But for Randy, worrying about the money was like fingering familiar Braille. And besides, he had a vet—Dr. Ed Migneco—who treated all of Stray Rescue's dogs at cost. Most of the time for less.

"The problems always work themselves out in the end," he said once the Chow rested on blankets in the back of the bus. "I'm not really a very spiritual person, but I believe in fate. Or something. I mean, if you do something good, something really good, not *because* it's good but because it's the right thing to do, then it always works out in the end.

"Always."

Chapter Three

Distant Instinct

Gray covered everything in the warehouse, from the rafters to the walls to the packed-earth floor. Dirty steel. Cindered dust. Grizzled light. Even the air was tin-drum hollow, so the flapping of pigeons and wind-ripped tin shingles lingered in space with no place to land.

Randy had come to the warehouse every day since rescuing Noel on that windy night before Christmas, and like most of the places he went—railroad yards, damp alleys, industrial barrens—this one stared at him with cool-eyed contempt, and he hated how he felt when he caught it looking. The trick was not to look back, not to let on; that way he stayed focused.

And he had to stay focused. If he didn't, he wouldn't save them. If he didn't save them, they would die, and they would haunt him, track him everywhere he went, until every ounce of his sense of worth ran screaming for the hills.

"Anybody here?"

Randy's words careened off the rafters. He followed them as they bounced from wall to wall like balls being thrown by ghosts. He wore a canvas coat and thick-soled boots, and when he sat down on the rusted rim of a truck tire in the middle of the floor, he shoved his hands in his pockets. A rat darted into the wall.

"This place gives me the creeps."

Except for the row houses across the street and the Can Man Recycling two blocks up, the buildings on Chouteau Street were deserted. On one side of the warehouse, a lifeless factory; on the other, an old truck yard. In back, three Quonset huts, empty since World War II, bordered a plain of utility towers, railroad yards, and lone saplings.

Inside the warehouse, late-morning winter sun streamed in through an open door onto a floor pockmarked by old fires. In the corner by the door, cobwebs hung like mosquito netting over a makeshift bed of wooden pallets covered by old blankets, sleeping bags, and newspaper. Next to the bed, on an overturned cardboard box, were a water-soaked Bible, a red plastic comb, and a camping manual for Scouts that explained how to carry a bedroll, tie knots, and build a fire on logs or large rocks.

On the ground next to the bed lay a faded piece of lined notebook paper. "March 26th: To review means to look again. I review before a test to remind myself of the important facts and concepts I want to remember. April 23rd: I have the power to control my perceptions. I am a positive thinker. I know I can do something when I put my mind to it. This helps me perceive myself in a positive way."

Randy stared at the bed as he fingered a plastic bag of braunschweiger, the lard-laced Midwestern version of liver pâté.

"Someone actually lives here," he said. "This stuff"—he waved at the bed of pallets with the hand holding the Baggie—"isn't used anymore. It must have belonged to someone who's gone, but there *is* someone living out in those things." He moved his eyes to the open doors and the Quonset huts looming beyond.

The Quonset huts, three corrugated metal caves shaped like small airplane hangars, sat beyond a field of weeds in back of the warehouse. While Randy had pushed himself as far as the overgrown pavement in front of the structures, he'd never gone inside.

Loose sheet metal banged against the roof in a gust of wind. Pigeons exploded from their hiding places in the rafters, and Randy hunched over as if protecting himself from thunder.

His eyes rolled up to the roof, then to the makeshift bed, then back out to the Quonset huts. The toe of his boot tapped the ground.

"They know I'm here," he said. "It just takes a little time for them to come out."

His hand bounced up and down on his knee as his boot tapped the ground, and his eyes darted back and forth across the dead space.

He crushed a cigarette into the dry floor under his boot. He looked at the door again.

"They're afraid, but they'll come eventually. They always do."

So he closed his eyes to the rats and the rafters and waited in silence for the dogs.

Compton showed up first. He usually did. As leader of the warehouse pack, he was the biggest, the most scarred, and the best able to decide for the rest whether the man who came every day with the Baggie of braunschweiger was the savior the others thought he might be.

"Hey, Compton, hey there." Randy knelt and stretched his hand out toward the dog, who stood in the doorway in a dusty ribbon of sun.

Compton's dense coat was the color of dirty yellow brick, but his broad shoulders and squared-off muzzle were darker, as if splashed. The deep furrow that ran down his forehead separated two cool amber eyes that never wavered from their focus.

Even though he was only about three years old, Compton was already an aging general, and he saw Randy as a threat to his hard-won authority. But like the six who hovered behind him outside in the snow, Compton was starving, so he stepped into the warmth of the warehouse and sat down five feet away. That was the agreed-upon distance.

"Don't make any moves toward him."

The first few minutes were crucial. The leader needed time to digest the situation, to establish his jurisdiction, to show the others behind him that he wouldn't rush up to the outstretched hand and take its offering with unquestioned submission. He would move in his own time, and the others would follow. Randy and he danced the same set of steps every day.

Compton's dark nose scanned the air until it locked in on the meat. His hind legs came up from the ground and his eyes stayed fixed on Randy. His tail didn't wag. His ears didn't snap forward. He didn't lunge for the meat as his malnourished body screamed for him to do. Every move he made was calculated to show Randy that he feared nothing, relished nothing, needed nothing at all.

Even though his eyes held their aggressive gaze, they couldn't veil the physical and emotional stresses that gnawed away at his confidence. For one, a broken back leg and starvation were eroding his stamina. For another, he found himself giving in more and more to Randy, who, because he supplied food, was proving himself the more effective provider.

"It's okay, Compton, I understand."

Randy watched Compton pull into himself and try to stare down the whispered assurances as if they were threats. It was the only thing that ensured his safety and that of the pack behind him.

Compton's sovereignty and his ability to survive in the wild were founded on what most dogs lost long ago: the ability to survive free of human help. But Compton was a product of domestication, so his desire to flee danger clashed with his desire to be cared for. As a result, he lived his life in a dense tangle of fear, because hunger pushed him unwillingly toward food that distant instinct told him he should have caught himself.

And every day, as Compton moved in on the meat, Randy tried to clear the trackless waste between them and tell Compton that he, too, was afraid of things.

Once the leader lapped up the first scraps of meat, dirt and all, Katlin, a small female Chow mix, trotted in, followed by a yellow female, Sunny, and three males, Midnight, Taz, and Bashful. Randy named dogs after nothing in particular, but he gave every dog a name. As they scattered across the floor of the warehouse, they watched Randy like students watching the clock.

"Hey gang," Randy said as he flung meat scraps toward them. He started each morning out with the "good stuff"—braun-schweiger, canned cat food, whatever steak was in his freezer—because he wanted them to think he was a successful hunter who was willing to share the prey. That way, one by one, they'd come to see him as the most efficient stalker, the best provider, the strongest leader—the one most likely to protect and feed them.

Sunshine hobbled into the warehouse last. She was a lithe yellow-haired Shepherd mix with fawn-brown eyes, cloudy and anxious. Like the others, she was thin and she limped on legs matted with burrs. Unlike the rest, she had a swollen belly that disguised her thinness, and she wiggled closer to Randy than the others as her tail wagged back and forth like a rudder.

"She's the weakest female in the pack right now," Randy said as he held a piece of meat out toward her on the tip of his finger. "She's at the bottom of the hierarchy, because she's pregnant and physically weak. She's vulnerable, and she knows it. That's why she lets me get so close."

Sunshine stretched her neck out toward him and sniffed at the meat, but as Randy moved his fingers toward her, she pranced back and away.

"She's not ready yet, but soon. Very soon." He let the meat fall to the ground.

When Randy first came to the warehouse after he rescued Noel, Sunshine and Midnight usually paired off, unconcerned in their youth about pack politics. But when Sunshine got pregnant and the growing pups inside her slowed her down, she couldn't keep up with the pack, and Midnight left his former playmate behind. Sunshine, increasingly alone, spent more and more time close to Randy, which meant more and more she broke pack rules.

"It takes a long time to gain their trust, and sometimes—most of the time—you have to take advantage of their weaknesses," Randy said. "People always ask me, 'How do you catch dogs that don't want to be caught?' and all I can say is that you can't *catch* them. It's not like they're viruses or crooks or something. They have to want to come with you."

He zeroed in on Sunshine's dejection, which was growing with her belly. Like all of the dogs', her emotional scaffolding paralleled that of insecure human teenagers who longed for praise, acceptance, and the safety of belonging. The dogs suffered heartbreak and depression, shame and grief. The natural need to be part of a group and the thousands of years of manipulative breeding that had made them dependent pets left them vulnerable to isolation, to the terror of being alone. They clung desperately to relationships that they hoped would last.

At the same time, they weren't animals raised on daily bowls of dog food, immunized and groomed and coddled in human homes. They didn't nuzzle, didn't play catch, didn't come when called. They were street dogs, scrappy and cynical survivors who were so skittish or aggressive or emotionally confused that they often defecated uncontrollably at the touch of human beings.

While Randy could have set a trap and forced Sunshine into a cage, the trauma would only have shoved her further into the abyss of twisted, instinctual fear. So rescue wasn't a matter of *catching* her; it was a matter of overcoming her untutored distrust and convincing her that the human pack was a safe place to be.

"The way I rescued Noel wasn't the right way," Randy mumbled as he fished another dab of meat out of the bag. "But at the time, I felt I had no choice."

He tossed the meat toward Sunshine, and she caught it on the fly.

"You are my Sunshine, my only Sunshine."

As Randy sang to her, Sunshine cocked her head. At the far edges of the warehouse, Compton and the rest of the pack looked on.

In 1993, the American Society of Mammologists decided that because the genetic difference between wolves and dogs was so small, about 0.2 percent or less, they should be classified as members of the same species. "Dogs are gray wolves," stated Robert K. Wayne, an evolutionary biologist at the University of California, Los Angeles, in his paper "Molecular Evolution of the Dog Family."

Because the minuscule genetic shift from wolf to dog began sometime between 14,000 and 100,000 years ago, we can only theorize how it happened. Some researchers believe that humans may have captured wolf pups and raised them as pets; any aggressive behavior or show of dominance by the wolves as they matured probably meant death or banishment from the human pack.

Consequently, only those wolves who continued docile, puppylike behavior into adulthood were allowed to live and breed, passing on their more submissive traits; over thousands of years, the domesticated dog came into being.

Others believe that wolves may have domesticated themselves.

Brave wolves, meaning in this context those most tolerant of people, may have started following human camps for the food scraps they provided, while their less brave brethren kept their distance and continued an autonomous legacy. Whatever genes, enzymes, or proteins made the brave wolves more "friendly" would then have been passed on to their offspring, until eventually what was once an aggressive, intuitive, 125-pound gray wolf became a docile, helpless seven-pound Toy Poodle.

Whatever happened, domesticated dogs are now classified as *Canis lupus familiaris,* a subspecies of the gray wolf. Some evolutionary biologists even believe that dogs are simply *Canis lupus.*

But domesticated dogs, even those born on the streets, lack many of the physical, emotional, and political characteristics of wolves, which would allow them to thrive in the wild. For example, conventional thought about the makeup of wolf packs suggests that the pack is a highly structured political body that depends on the absolute commitment of every individual for the body as a whole to survive. An alpha pair mates and administers the rules, which all of the pack members follow.

Most wolf packs are small, however, and recent research by Dr. David Mech, the senior research scientist at the Northern Prairie Wildlife Research Center University of Minnesota Field Station, indicates that they are generally made up of a mating pair and its offspring at various stages of maturity. Mech found that the small pack is simply a family unit and that what have been called "dominance" and "submission" in the past only really represent the I-know-more-than-you relationship that occurs naturally between parents and offspring. In other words, the younger the wolf, the more "submissive" he or she is to the older wolves in the pack. As he grows, the young wolf becomes more and more "dominant" until he leaves the family unit—usually within three years—to start his own pack. The term "alpha pair," Mech suggests, is a misnomer, which should be replaced with "parents of the pack."

In larger groups, with several families living together, a social contract is enforced by an alpha male and female who "dominate" the rest. They are the ones who decide when it's time to hunt, when it's time to rest, when it's time to play. Usually, only they mate; they generally eat first and distribute food to their offspring. The rest of the wolves each hold their own rank, from the second-in-command betas to the weakest, most vulnerable omegas.

But the alphas aren't alphas because they hunger for glory, and the omegas aren't omegas because their coat is off-color. Each rank has its own jobs, its own responsibilities, its own importance to the pack. While only the parent pair produces offspring, for example, each member of the group takes its turn feeding, cleaning, and playing with the pups. Likewise, when the pack hunts, some track, some chase, some attack. The pack, by design, runs like a well-disciplined military battalion.

Domesticated dogs lack many of these organizational skills because they've been bred to live with humans in a pack where they are always the omegas. In the human pack, their survival—and the passage of their genes to offspring—does not necessarily depend on their ability to hunt prey or reproduce healthy offspring or understand complicated pack hierarchy. They are not mentally or physically designed to be on their own.

When Sunshine gulped down the dry food Randy poured into a bowl for her, she stretched out near his feet, legs extended, as if drying her toenails. He looked down at the thin yellow dog who looked so much like Noel and shook his head. Had Randy known Noel was part of this pack, he would have waited to rescue her.

"She was so scared. She was separated from this pack, it was her family, and she didn't understand what was happening to her," he said.

Gaining the trust of street dogs, especially those running alone, might take less than a week. But wild dogs in a pack feel sheltered by their numbers; to win them over takes hundreds of hours of watching them, feeding them, earning the right to be part of the group. Each member has secrets to tell, but it sometimes takes years to pry them out.

The night Randy rescued Noel, he immediately recognized in her the symptoms of wildness: the denial of eye contact; the uncontrollable shaking; the misinterpretation of his gestures of solace for those of threat. As he sat with her that night in his garage, every time he tried to get close to her, she cowered and rolled on her back and urinated on herself in fear.

Randy made up a bed for himself in the garage, turned on a space heater, and listened to the wind as Noel turned her back and shuddered in silence. He sang to her. He talked to her. He told her about his rescues, about his therapist, about how old he thought God might be.

"See, I had to think of her as a wild animal. Milk Bones meant nothing to her. Squeaky toys meant nothing to her. Kind words meant nothing to her. None of the how-to's in dog-training books applied. The only way to get her to accept me was to prove that I was the alpha, the leader, in this new pack."

He raided his refrigerator—filet mignon leftovers, French cheese, pâté—then ate the food in front of her as he talked. He talked for hours. At some point, he tossed her a scrap of cheese, but she scurried into another corner of the garage as if he'd thrown a bucket of water at her instead.

Randy kept talking. The next time he threw out a piece of food, she flinched but didn't run, just eyed the scrap with suspicion. The third piece made her nose twitch. The fourth coaxed her head forward.

Finally she stepped out of the corner and snatched at the scrap. She was starving, and once she tasted food, she wasn't going to stop. Randy tossed more scraps out, each one closer to himself than the last. He reeled her in, bite by bite, and by dawn, she was asleep at his side.

"On their first night off the street, they fall into this deep sleep. I love to watch it happen. It's probably the first time in their lives that they're warm and safe and full.

"I don't know how long I sat there and watched her sleep. It's kind of like watching something . . . being born. You know?"

He laughed sarcastically, as if the words had been muttered by some other sentimental fool. Sunshine's head popped up, and Randy smiled down at her.

"I don't want Sunshine to have to go through that. I don't want to trap her or trick her into leaving this place. I want her to come on her own."

He stood up and poured dog chow into three other bowls scattered around the floor. The rest of the pack waited until he was a safe distance away. Then they lunged for the food.

It was Randy's favorite part of every day, when the pack was done eating and relaxed in the warehouse all around him. Taz, the group's lookout, sat perched by the open door as Katlin, Midnight, Bashful, and Sunny lounged in shafts of warm light and licked at wounds. Compton, whose leadership hinged on detachment, watched them from his corner.

"They're letting me hang out, letting me be part of the pack. Sometimes I think I could sit here forever."

But he couldn't. He had to get back to the grooming shop, and there were dogs to take to the vet's, foster homes to find, voice mail crammed to capacity with calls to return. Volunteers, money, e-mails. They banged in his head for attention.

As he stood up from his post on the tire rim, the dogs' ears went to full alert. It was time to go. Taz, still posted by the door, left first. Midnight, Bashful, Katlin, and Sunny trotted out behind him. Compton, who usually guarded the rear, stood up slowly, his eyes riveted on Sunshine and Randy as if warning Sunshine to leave and Randy not to follow.

Sunshine peered up at Randy and tilted her head. Then her eyes turned to the open door where Compton waited. Randy pulled out a cigarette and followed Sunshine through the door.

He walked a path that had been worn through brittle dead weeds at the height of late-August corn, and that ran from the warehouse to the Quonset huts out back. As he stepped onto the asphalt in front of the three buildings, Randy stopped, scanned the ground, and then pointed to a pile of dead pigeons.

"This," he said, nudging the frozen carcasses with his foot, "is why I come back here day after day."

Randy looked up at the sun, then over to the Quonset huts, then back down to the birds. Out on Chouteau, two men layered in coats pushed squeaking grocery carts full of aluminum cans up the sidewalk toward Can Man Recycling.

"The dogs can't hunt. They don't know how. If it wasn't for human garbage, they'd starve. I've had X rays done on dogs who had their own puppies' bones tearing up their insides, because they were so hungry, they *ate* them."

Randy flung his cigarette down and smashed it out with his boot.

"I've found dogs beaten, run on treadmills, fed gunpowder, and chained in the sun to make them mean. I've found dogs with broken backs. I've found dogs wrapped in heavy chains and padlocks. I've found dogs with slit throats. I've found dogs buried alive just to make them mean, only they've been domesticated not to be mean, so emotionally they're all screwed up.

"Then they're abandoned. They get thrown out of cars, dumped off bridges—the lucky ones just get shot. The unlucky ones have to fend for themselves, only they don't know how. Sometimes they're able to join a pack, but that only means they get to watch each other die. Usually of starvation."

The shopping carts clattered up the road.

"I know I should feel more sorry for people. I know I should care more about abused children and battered women and the state of health care in this country, but there are other people worrying about those things. Nobody is worrying about these dogs out here who don't know how to hunt or how to fend for themselves or how to survive on their own."

He pointed down at the pile of dead pigeons.

"The dogs caught these birds. Somehow, they reached back into their far-off instinct and learned how to hunt them, but once they caught them, they didn't know how to get through the feathers to the meat." He jabbed his boot into the pile. "They didn't know how to eat them."

And there they lay, a rotting monument to domestication.

Randy shielded his eyes and watched the pack jog single file along the railroad tracks in back of the Quonset huts. As they shrank from view, Sunshine, far behind the others, stopped and looked back at the warehouse.

Chapter Four

How to Get a Life
Without Even Trying

Randy jabbed his fork at the grilled salmon and watched flakes of pink flesh scatter across the plate. As a waiter passed with a tray of drinks for the jazz trio assembling on the small stage behind him, Randy glanced up, puffed out his cheeks, and pushed the fish in large circles around on his plate. Next to him, Paul Humbert balanced his chair on its rear legs.

"I used to be more like Paul," Randy said.

Paul raised his eyebrows and surveyed Randy's stretched-out black sweater and jeans as if they hung from an off-season rack. Randy didn't look up, just shoved the fish around on his plate.

"What he means," Paul said as he dropped the chair onto all fours, "is that he used to be normal."

Randy pushed the salmon until it slid over the edge. "Normal." He whispered the word like the name of a deity, like something he worshipped from afar.

He used to sport a Mohawk, listen to punk rock, and dream about the day when he would live on a California beach. He and Paul owned a town house in the gentrified Lafayette Square neighborhood just south of downtown St. Louis. At the heart of the neighborhood was a park where people, or the people they hired, exercised their Standard Poodles and Afghan Hounds. Business at his grooming shop boomed, social diversions were plentiful, and life sped forward, with Depeche Mode keeping time.

But that was all before Bonnie, who crossed his path one day like a one-float parade of ill fate.

She was a Collie mix. When Randy found her in front of his grooming shop, she was so thin that her spine poked out of her back. From this hung her pregnant belly, like a duffel bag stuffed with socks. When she walked, she swayed; everything about her was askew—one eye swollen shut, one ear flopped down, one leg jacked up in a sideways V.

When she first saw Randy, she plopped to the sidewalk and cocked her head as if waiting for permission to follow.

"She was pathetic," Randy said. "I mean, I'd always loved dogs. I already had three who were former strays, but I knew Paul would have a fit if I brought another one home. But he was away on a trip, so I let her follow me home."

His first call was to the city animal control department, which informed him that the stray, like 70 percent of the others brought in, would be put down because she "wasn't healthy." His next call, to the Humane Society of Missouri, was equally dispiriting: a pregnant dog just couldn't be adopted out. His trip with her to the vet the next day offered no solutions either.

"The vet—it wasn't Dr. Ed—was really mean. He acted like I'd brought in a dirty mop for him to look at or something. I mean, when I asked him if he had any clients who might want her, he didn't even bother answering my question. I was like this door-to-door salesman with a product nobody wanted."

The vet announced that the dog, while not feral, had been alone on the streets for a long time and was probably too weak from malnourishment to survive her impending delivery. Randy would have to take her temperature rectally every day and watch for signs of labor. Because the thought of watching for signs of labor sparked the first flares of a panic attack, Randy wrapped her up in her blanket and fled.

He named her Bonnie not so much because he wanted to form a relationship as because he needed to call her something other than "the dog." But a bond, from her point of view, formed anyway. No matter where he went in the house, she followed, her toenails clacking like typewriter keys on the wood floor behind him. She seemed torn between the need to keep him in sight and the need to breathe.

The first time he left the town house for the grooming shop, Bonnie pulled down the window blinds in an effort to follow, and every day for the next week, Randy came home to new evidence of her fear of being alone: sheets torn from the beds, clothes ripped from their hangers, windows coated with her frantic slobber, wood floors scarred by her pacing. He wondered, at one point, if she might be possessed.

Randy found her exaggerated devotion disconcerting. She didn't act like other dogs. The Golden Retrievers he groomed in the shop didn't wail as if in pain when their owners left and didn't act like obsessed lovers when they returned. When friends came to the town house, Bonnie hid in the basement and shook, but when Randy walked in the door, she folded her body into a wiggling figure eight of exhilaration, and sometimes her greetings of melodramatic yips, elaborate leaps, and contorted body wags turned so frenzied that he worried she'd damage the growing puppies inside her. She was just one body, but it was like being greeted by a maddened crowd.

After a few weeks of Bonnie's separation-anxiety destruction, Randy started hauling her to the shop with him during the day. At first, he put her in a crate in the back room, but her howls of despair upset the other dogs and nearly drove his employees to strike, so he moved her up into the front room to the only spot where she seemed at peace—beside his grooming table, where she could see every move he made.

Randy felt shackled to a devoted slave, an overly sensitive, desperate subject. During the day, inside her crate, Bonnie gauged where he was in the room and kept her black nose pressed against the grate. At night, while he pored over books on dog training, she lay prostrate at his feet like a victim of devotion.

As her delivery neared, Randy slept with Bonnie on a futon in the basement. But she had nightmares and whined in her sleep, and when her growing body rolled from one side of the couch to the other, it was like sleeping on a stretch of bad sea.

It was obvious that Bonnie had been abused. Randy was the only person who could get within breathing distance of her, and even then, she shied from every quick gesture he made. So he moved slowly, talked quietly, acted as though the world were a much kinder place than she imagined. He gave her gourmet dog food, smoked pig ears, vitamins, and a rhinestone-studded leash. Because he found himself more and more worried about her health, he bought an air filter so she wouldn't have to breathe in his cigarette smoke.

While he read every book he could find on dogs, there was a difference between Bonnie and the well-kept animals pictured on the glossy pages. They were beautiful and obedient and trusting; Bonnie was sickly and stubbornly afraid. They were bred purposefully to produce dogs who looked and behaved just like them. Who knew what grew inside Bonnie's swollen belly?

She always kept her eyes on him; she watched him, he was sure, when he slept. He was her hero, her infatuation, her soul mate. By the time she went into violent labor almost three weeks later, Randy felt like a matinee idol.

"Who owns the dog having puppies?"

The vet technician stood halfway in and halfway out of Exam Room One with fear and annoyance competing for control of her face.

Randy's eyes widened. He shot a look across the waiting room to his friend and neighbor Janet Carp, whom he'd yanked away from work when Bonnie's labor started earlier that afternoon.

Janet leaned forward and pointed at Randy. "You do," she mouthed.

"I do," Randy repeated as he pulled his gaze away from Janet and toward the technician. "I mean, I guess I do. She was a stray . . ."

The technician waved him toward her. "Get in here, quick."

Randy looked at Janet, shook his head, and pointed his finger at his chest.

"But . . ."

"Sir!"

Randy stumbled into the exam room and saw Bonnie's body on the table, belly laid open. Adrenaline, nausea, and the urge to flee sailed electrically through Randy's chest, but this was more than a stress-induced, caffeine-laced, fluorescently lit panic attack; this was fear, blinking away, real and plugged in for the night.

"Is she . . . ?"

The technician thrust something into Randy's hand. A deformed guinea pig wrapped in white, wet tissue paper.

"Shake it," the vet instructed without turning away from Bonnie, "and rub it, rub it hard."

Randy looked down at the thing in his hands. It was slimy, whatever it was, and cold.

"Shake it, like this." The vet held another one of the things in his hand and jerked it forward into the air. "Then rub it, like this. You've got to get it breathing."

Randy looked down at the zoological horror in his hands. "Breathing?"

"Hurry up, there's more."

Randy held the thing out as far away from his body as he could and jiggled it in the air.

"Harder. You've got to get it breathing."

He jiggled it harder and rubbed the handful of mush. But the technician yanked it out of his hands and pushed another one of the creatures toward him. He shook and he rubbed. Another came at him. He shook and he rubbed. Then another came, and another. Gooey UFOs flew at him from all directions.

"Janet!"

When she ran through the doorway, she gasped. "Oh my God." Randy tossed her one of the things. "Shake it and rub it."

"What?"

"Rub it hard. You've got to get it breathing."

It was like a morbid game of Hot Potato. The vet pulled the things out of Bonnie's body, thrust them at the technician, who passed them to Randy, who tossed them to Janet.

They shook and rubbed, shook and rubbed. They shook and rubbed until their arms ached and bloody, primordial muck dried under their fingernails and sweat ran down their faces. Another came and another. It was like working an understaffed assembly line, and then, when they thought they couldn't shake or rub one more of the slippery little aliens . . . they stopped coming. And it was over.

The vet and the assistant stood staring at the blood and gunk around them as Janet crumpled into the wall. Randy stared at Bonnie.

"Is she . . . ?"

The vet nodded. "She's alive."

And around them, on the floor, in the corners, and under the chairs, lay thirteen whimpering, beached baby blobs.

Several weeks later, on Paul's birthday, the town house filled with friends and family members. There were garlic-stuffed mushroom caps, barbecued tuna steaks, and enough banana daiquiris to intoxicate Guam. There were helium balloons at the ceiling and confetti on the floor; Cher's greatest hits filled the air. Because Randy had planned the party months before, his absence from the revels was noted.

"He's downstairs," Paul told the guests as he rolled his eyes toward the closed basement door. "He's been down there for weeks."

The guest followed his eyes.

"He found this dog in front of the grooming shop, who delivered thirteen puppies," Paul said, "and three days later, the vet tells Randy that she can't nurse them because she developed some kind of infection in her boobs."

Downstairs, Randy heard the muffled conversation. He would have gestured obscenely toward the ceiling if he hadn't had a puppy cradled in his arms.

"It's called mastitis!" he yelled at the ceiling.

When the vet first muttered the word "mastitis" at the clinic, it sounded innocuous, like the name of a sailor's knot or a rare strain of food poisoning indigenous to cruise ships. But the vet was avoiding eye contact. He explained that mastitis was an infection of the mammary glands: Bonnie wouldn't be able to nurse the puppies.

Several moments of silence crawled by and left a slimy trail of denial behind them. The vet, still avoiding eye contact with Randy, cleared his throat.

"You'll have to hand-feed all thirteen puppies, every two hours, around the clock until they're weaned."

Several more moments of silence.

"And you'll have to weigh them and stimulate them to defecate after every feeding."

More silence.

"Did you hear me?"

Randy raised his eyebrows. "For how long?"

"Six weeks."

Randy bought thirteen baby bottles, several supersized economy barrels of powdered puppy formula, and thirteen different shades of toenail polish, so he could tell the puppies apart. Then he called his shop and told his employees he'd be at home, in the basement, for the next six weeks if they needed him for anything.

Every two hours, Randy sterilized the bottles, mixed up the formula, and then fed each puppy, weighed each puppy, and stimulated each puppy to defecate. Some of the puppies were too weak to suck, so he had to force-feed them with a tube pushed into their stomachs. By the time he got done with the thirteenth puppy, it was time for the feeding, weighing, pooping, and peeing to start all over again.

Keeping every puppy alive allowed him only fifteen-minute naps grabbed here and there, and it didn't take long for mind-numbing sleeplessness to distort all sense of time and place. He slowly let go of the rest of the world. He quit answering the phone, stopped thinking of work, shut down his desire to shower or shave, and as hours turned into days and days into weeks, the rock that was once his self-interest turned into a mushy bog focused entirely on three increasingly hyperactive laundry hampers: "To Be Fed," "Already Fed," and "To Be Pooped & Weighed."

Stress girdled his brain like barbed wire . . . have to feed the puppies, have to feed the puppies, have to feed the puppies . . . and soon the stench and sounds of the subterranean squalor drove most sympathetic well-wishers far away. From time to time Paul opened the door and threw bags of Burger King down to him, then slammed the door back shut.

Randy's friend Peggy Hightower dropped supplies for him every day and helped with the feedings. She designed a spreadsheet, on which he was instructed to record every feeding, weighing, pooping, and peeing, but it took too much time to fill out, and Randy used it to clean up puppy poop instead. When Peggy explained that it was for his own benefit, he flung a hamburger at her and told her to go away.

Eventually he figured out that he could cut down on the poop-and-pee time by holding a just-fed puppy out toward Bonnie as he picked up another with his free hand. In assembly-line fashion, Bonnie licked the outstretched infant, stimulating it to defecate, as Randy sang show tunes to stay awake—"There's *no* business like *show* business like *no* business I *know*"—and then fed the next puppy in line.

Despite the teamwork and the few extra minutes of sleep it provided, Randy felt reality slide sideways. The outside world didn't exist, except as something he'd read about in a novel long ago, and when it did intrude, as when his mother came over from her house next door, he couldn't make out any of the details.

"You've got to stop this, Randy." Hazy, faded words came at him through the fog. "This is craziness. . . . You can't go on like this. . . ." His mother's face was distorted, as if under water. "You're not eating. . . . It smells awful down here. . . ." Bonnie was hiding in the corner. "You've got to do something with these animals."

"Mom?"

"The neighbors all think you're crazy. It's not just me . . ."

"Hey, Mom?"

"And Paul, poor Paul, what about him? And what about the shop? And what about—"

"Mom."

"—Paul's birthday?" She paused and caught her breath. "What?"

"Did you breast-feed me?"

"What?"

"I said, 'Did you breast-feed me?' "

"What?"

"You didn't, did you?"

He didn't mean it as an accusation, just wanted confirmation so he knew how to calibrate his cosmic alignment with the pups, but his mother disappeared at some misty point—"Peeeo-ple, people who need peeeo-ple"—leaving in her wake a casserole. Which he ate with his fingers.

As Paul unwound the story for his guests upstairs, they tossed hoots and hollers down the basement steps.

"Mommie dearest, get up here," someone called in mock soprano.

"Is the wet nurse too busy to come up and play?"

Down in the abyss, ankle deep in puppy poop, Randy wondered if he had indeed lost his mind. Maybe at that moment, he only *imagined* he was surrounded by thirteen wiggling, crying creatures from outer space when in reality he was being fitted for a straitjacket.

"Get a life!" someone called down the stairs.

Randy looked over at Bonnie, whose nose was pressed up against one of the laundry baskets, and she returned his gaze with an artless, soft-brown innocence. Attentive though she was to the brood she couldn't feed, she still stared at him as if he were God. Whenever he came near her, she rolled on her back as if offering herself as a sacrifice, and when he fed the puppies, she let the full weight of her head rest on his lap, seeming to match her breathing to his own.

None of this was her fault. None of it. She hadn't asked to be abused or abandoned. She couldn't fight her ignorance anymore than she could fight off the male strays who probably gang-raped her when she was in heat. Bonnie needed him, and he realized that he had never had anything need him so much before.

Get a life?

Randy motioned for Bonnie to stay put as he staggered toward the basement stairs. From above, he could hear the deep *bump, bump, bump* of music and the laughs of clean-shaven, well-dressed, carefree people. Even though he hadn't slept, showered, or seen sunlight in three weeks, he pulled himself up toward the party, one step at a time.

He had something to say.

As he opened the door, the light stung his eyes. He stood there squinting, swaying back and forth as every eye in the room swerved toward him.

"What's *that*?" someone whispered.

Someone else laughed nervously. Someone else turned down the music.

Randy stood and swayed and glared at the people in his living room. Then he pointed his index finger at his chest. Then he screwed up his face. He was going to speak.

"I *have* a life!"

He dropped his hand from his chest and stood there as the bellowed words splashed off the ceiling, slid down the walls, and cuffed every unhinged jaw in the room.

"I *have* a life," he whispered.

Then he turned and headed back down to where Bonnie, tail wagging, waited for him at the foot of the steps.

"I lost friends over that," Randy said. "Everyone thought I was a freak. But I didn't choose it. Everyone acted like I chose to find this pregnant dog, that I chose for her to have thirteen puppies, that I chose for her to get mastitis. But I didn't choose any of it. I mean, what options did I have?"

After the puppies were weaned, they, like Bonnie, followed Randy everywhere. He taught them how to climb the stairs, and soon they raced from the basement out the back door where Paul, who called them the Children, taught them how to swim in a plastic wading pool.

As they grew, Randy bought them a portable, six-foot-high pen, but whenever he walked away from it, the puppies followed in the cage en masse.

"It was a really weird relationship that Bonnie and I developed. She needed me; she depended on me for everything. I loved that dog, and we went through hell together. I finally found homes for her and the puppies, but giving them away was the hardest thing I've ever done in my life."

From that point on, he noticed strays everywhere: in the parks, in the alleys, in the streets. He found them limping along the highways, hiding under bridges, and running into vacant buildings. He started picking them up.

"I couldn't *not* pick them up," he said. "I saw Bonnie's face in all of them."

Sometimes, when he chased one into a junkyard, or an empty field, or the crumbling shell of a long-closed hospital, church, or school, he found whole packs and litters of puppies at various stages of life and death. At first, he thought the Pit Bulls and the Shepherds and the Doberman-Mastiff mixes were all abandoned pets, but he soon learned that when he stopped and called to them, he got one of three reactions: they limped like thankful beggars up to the bus; they inched toward him, grabbed whatever he had in his hand, and then ran away; or they eyed him aloofly from a distance and never came near.

He assumed that some of them were just scared and chalked up the fear to abuse. But then one of the vets he haunted—there were only eight clinics in the entire city—guessed that they might be feral dogs, born on the streets.

"That blew my mind. I had no idea dogs lived wild in the city."

At first Randy would pick them up and rush them to the closest vet clinic and pay the bill with a credit card. One dog with heartworm cost him half a week's income to heal. Eye infections cost $60; spay or neuter, $100; mange, $150 and up. Those were just the basics and didn't include broken backs or mutilated tails or cancers or gunshot wounds or whipworms.

Once the dog was healed, Randy got on the phone and called everyone he knew—friends, clients, neighbors—until he found it a home.

"I begged, I cried, I threatened, you name it," he said. "And they all said the same thing: 'You can't save them all.' But when someone said that to me, I put a bow around the dog's neck and presented it to that person as a gift, so they *couldn't* refuse."

Within a year, Randy found himself broke, excommunicated from more and more vet clinics, and an object of increasing concern to Paul, his mother, and his closest friends.

"He wasn't any fun to be around anymore," said one longtime acquaintance. "All he did was try to give us these dogs he found. Every time you got near him, you had to sit through these long stories about how many stray dogs there were and about how nobody cared and blah-blah-blah. We all thought he'd had a nervous breakdown or something."

But as Randy's social circle frayed at the edges, he found himself in the middle of a tightly bound web of "volunteers"—people who helped him and introduced him to other people who introduced him to others—which eventually included an attorney who helped Randy form a not-for-profit organization and allowed him to accept donations.

Because he had depleted most of his creativity in naming the dogs—they were easier to give away if they had the perfect name—he decided to call the group Stray Rescue. And while the new organization's first donations came mainly from the wallets of Randy and his three-member "board of directors," being the founder of a group registered at the Missouri secretary of state's office gave him a temporary sense of justification. It also attracted the attention of a city vet, Dr. Edward Migneco, who volunteered to treat all of Stray Rescue's dogs at cost.

"Dr. Ed just turned up out of nowhere and offered to help," Randy said. "Without him, we'd be sunk."

One day soon after Randy gave Bonnie and the puppies away, he and his mother sat in the backyard with their feet in the wading pool.

"She asked me if I had learned my lesson," Randy said, and then he laughed. "I told her that the only thing I had learned was that my basement wasn't big enough."

Chapter Five

The Game Dogs

Gray-washed winter morning. Soot-washed winter streets. Cold and flat as iron, it was a standard, restless day. One hour before the grooming shop opened, Randy dropped food at the warehouse on Chouteau, then at an entrance ramp of I-40 where several other dogs spent their nights in the weeds, then at an oil-storage tower where he'd seen two Akitas and a Chow several days before. As he headed back, he flipped open his cell phone and checked the Stray Rescue line at the shop.

Beeeep. "Randy, I tried, but this Pit Bull I'm fostering is tearing up my house. . . ."

Beeeep. "Hi, Randy, it's Dr. Ed. Hate to tell you this, but the Chow you brought in has a bad case of mange and heartworm. . . ."

Beeeep. "Randy, somebody called me yesterday about two stray Rottweilers who are attacking cats in their neighborhood. . . ."

Beeeep. "Hi, Randy. I saw your web page and would like to adopt one of your dogs. I was wondering if you had any white ones with longish hair? That way it would look like the dog I already have. About thirty pounds, gentle, you know, and house-trained?"

Randy rolled his eyes, pulled the phone away from his ear, and stared at it as if the caller had asked for a dog who did dishes. He checked the last message.

Beeeep. "My name is, is, never mind, I, I, I have this dog, see. These kids, they, they, they, see, she was throwed off the bridge. I live by the river and I saw 'em. I got her in my garage, and she's, she's, bad off. Real bad. I live down by the river. Can you come quick?"

Randy shoved the cell phone in his coat pocket. People said anything when they had a pet they didn't want anymore: the last one told Randy she had found a stray Labrador in her backyard—a purebred, she assured him with pride. When Randy asked her how she knew it was a purebred, the woman sighed. "Because he's got *papers,*" she said.

Randy understood such desperate measures. People knew if they took a pet to any of the local shelters, its chance of walking out alive was about as good as a fish's on a sidewalk. Even if it was a purebred. Of the millions of animals in America's shelters on any given day, at least one-fourth are purebreds.

But most of the dogs Randy started picking up off the streets after Bonnie (everything in his life was now measured on a timeline of "before" and "after" Bonnie) weren't purebreds, not purebreds with legitimate papers, anyway. Most were genetic conglomerations of the breeds with the most potential for aggressive behavior—Pit Bull–Shepherds, Shepherd-Akitas, Chow-Shepherd-Doberman mixes—all hungry, all scarred, and all on a fruitless search for safety.

Most of the dogs weren't sterilized, in part because no veterinarians set up shop in poorer neighborhoods and in larger part because intact dogs displayed more aggression—a highly valued trait. But not even the biggest and meanest of the dogs Randy rescued were immune to disease, starvation, or the constant fear of living on the streets, and because they hadn't had cover so long, they often didn't recognize it when they found it. Even in the warmth and safety of a new home, they bit, they cowered, they circled in corners for hours on end. Some were hyperactive; others wallowed in depression. Most hid from humans. Most, at first, wouldn't eat.

After forming Stray Rescue, Randy read dog training books, interviewed shelter workers, and enlisted an animal behaviorist to help him exorcise the dogs' tortured psyches.

"All of that stuff helped, but the main thing I learned was to trust my own instincts," Randy said. "I knew these dogs were afraid, and I knew what it felt like and what they were afraid of. Hell, I owned a corner on fear. There isn't anything I didn't understand about their behavior."

Randy set up a system in which the rescued dogs were immediately sent, day or night, to Dr. Ed's clinic, where they were treated for their broken bones, eye infections, and mange. While they were at the clinic, Randy searched his volunteer list for a foster home where the dog could be "stashed" until he found a permanent placement.

But he required all foster and adoptive parents to fill out forms, sit through interviews, and agree to meet with a behaviorist if their dog got out of hand. Most of all, he tried to convince them that their dog's bad behavior was like the post-traumatic stress disorder experienced by humans after intense and prolonged fear. It wasn't that the dogs *liked* being mean.

As Randy drove the bus toward the grooming shop, he pulled the cell phone back out of his pocket and stared at it. The caller, an old woman, had said she found a dog thrown into the Mississippi. People would say anything.

But if he didn't go and get the dog, there'd be one more stray on the street, so he dialed the shop and told his employees that he'd be in late again.

"I'm headed down to the river," he said.

The massive McKinley Bridge was constructed by the Illinois Traction System in 1910 and once carried trains, wagons, and streetcars between the swarming restlessness on either bank of the Mississippi River, where lumberyards, cotton factories, and ice houses flourished on one side, stockyards, switch shops, and steel mills steamed on the horizon of the other, and ferries and mile-long lines of steamboats vied for space on the waterway in between. At one time, St. Louis was the third busiest port in the country, and the McKinley Bridge linked one side of America with the other.

Less than a century later, with most of the water traffic and industry gone and with the Mississippi so foul with oil spills and chemical leaks and fertilizer runoff that St. Louisans were advised not to fish there anymore, the bridge mainly served as a place for teenage trysts and suicide.

At its base, in the constant watercolor twilight of a nearby power plant, an old white house still stood. Gray dust from a gravel road powdered the willow and poplar trees in the front yard, and a chain-link fence with green plastic slats guarded plastic forest fauna, plastic No Trespassing signs, and plastic daisies whirling on sticks in the rancid breeze off the river.

The stretch of gravel road had once been a main artery along the levee, congested with cotton bales, towers of bricks, piles of lumber, and horse-drawn wagons loaded with cold barrels of beer from the breweries that clomped like thunder down the cobblestones. There were restaurants and hotels and hardware stores. There were sunburned German dockworkers and cattle and coal carts and tourists.

Now the street looked like a jungle airstrip. Except for the small white house, the only signs of human design were the power plant, an unused railroad track out back, and the empty corrugated husk of a steel mill down the road. That, and an old woman in the side yard who waved at Randy's bus as if flagging a cab in Manhattan.

"Over here! I'm over here!"

Randy pulled the bus over, and the old woman, dressed in a pink-and-orange muumuu with a green scarf tied around her hair, wagged her bony hands toward the garage behind the house. White dust kicked up from the gravel road swirled and settled around her.

"In there! She's in there!"

Randy jumped out, and the old woman clapped her hands and danced back and forth in the dust as if God himself had just landed.

"I knew you'd come. I knew it. I just *knew* it."

Randy glanced up at the arching metal-and-concrete latticework of the bridge across the road. Even from its lowest point, a long drop stretched between the bridge and the dark, rushing water below. If someone had climbed up there and dumped a dog off, Randy thought, it wasn't likely to have survived the fall. Not that that made any difference. He'd take the crazy old woman's dog anyway.

"She's in there," the old woman said again. She hopped up and down and jabbed a white, bony finger toward the garage. "They throwed her right off right there"—she pointed up at the bridge— "a gang of kids, I seen 'em, just throwed her right into the water"— her finger traced an arc down to the river—"and she washed up, and I fished her out and dragged her to the garage"—she waved back at the garage—"and I called you, because I heard of you and knew God would answer my prayers and send someone to help me, I just knew it, because they throwed that poor thing off the bridge. . . ."

Randy, who stood a foot taller than the old woman, swung his palms back and forth in the air to calm her. "It's okay. . . ."

As the old woman clasped her hands together as if in prayer, a black dog, a Labrador and Pit Bull mix with solid black eyes, trotted from the back of the yard and stopped at the corner of the house.

His eyes bracketed Randy like prey in a gun sight. His ears shot forward, his top lip curled up, and a low growl rumbled deep in his throat. As the growl erupted into a rapid-fire bark, the black dog pounced in place on stiff legs like a machine gun held by an invisible chain.

"Don't mind him," the old woman said, as the black dog's nose wrinkled and the fur on his back and tail bristled like a swatch of upturned nails. "He's just a little ornery. And no wonder. I can't tell you what these poor dogs go through 'round here. Just awful. But some of 'em get away. . . ."

The old woman turned and nodded her head at a small wooded area on the outside of the fence. The heads of several large dogs poked out from behind trees as they peered into the yard.

"I feed 'em best I can, but they're pretty scared of me."

The barking dogs' circle tightened around Randy.

"There's about ten of 'em that lives in the woods there. Poor things."

The old woman grabbed Randy's sleeve and pulled him toward the garage, past a row of dented garbage cans, a white Dodge Dart, and a line of aluminum pie tins filled with dog food. Randy tried to keep a fix on the dogs in the woods—scarred Pit Bulls, Shepherd mixes with torn ears, Rottweilers with mange—but with the old woman yanking at his sleeve and the black dog snapping at his boots, it was like being hauled through shark-infested water behind a small tugboat.

The old woman pulled a ring with two keys from her sweater pocket and rammed them both at the garage door lock several times before one slid in. As her head and shoulders disappeared through the door, the black dog grabbed at Randy's pant leg.

"Miss Dog? We're comin' in, Miss Dog. Don't be afraid. This man is here to help you. . . . Don't you worry. . . ."

A band of light poured into the interior and onto a golden Chow-Retriever mix lying on the floor. She lifted her head up and focused on the sound of the old woman's voice.

Randy closed the door on the barking dog's face and moved toward the dog on crouched legs.

"Hey, pretty girl, hey there."

The Chow's head rotated as if searching for the source of the words, and when she couldn't seem to find what she was looking for, she dropped her head back to the ground and whimpered. Scabs covered the tips of her velvet ears, and a row of hair mats with debris embedded in them clung to the side of her body like a litter of suckling pups. A white film covered one of her eyes, and as Randy stroked the indentation between her ears, she batted her tail on the ground.

"What happened to her eye?" Randy asked.

"They beat her with a big stick up there on the bridge before they throwed her in. I saw 'em do it. I would of yelled at 'em to stop, but, you know, they'd a come after me next."

"Who'd come after you next?"

"Can't talk about it. Varmints. Will she live? Can you save her?"

"I've got to get her to the vet," Randy said as he scooped up the Chow's limp body. He could feel long tracks of scabs on her body.

Outside, the black dog waited. When he saw Randy with the Chow in his arms, he resumed his stiff-legged bluster from a distance.

"You stop that now." The old woman rushed toward the dog and waved her hands at his face. "Stop that, you hear? Bad boy. Bad boy."

But the dog's eyes stayed clamped on Randy, and as he barked, the bounce of his body propelled him forward until Randy saw fleas popping from around his eyes and thin strings of saliva dripping from his teeth. The black dog snapped at the air and then at Randy's shadow and then at the leg of his pants.

"Stop that, now. You'll scare the man. Bad Boy. Bad boy . . ."

Randy yanked his knees up high, so his legs were less of a target. The old woman's scolds turned to shrieks.

"Bad dog! Bad dog! Stop that, hear me? Stop that now!"

Randy marched through the yard as the black dog circled and snapped, and the old woman circled and swatted at the air. When they reached the bus, he rested the Chow in the back as the black dog's teeth grabbed at his shins.

"Bad boy! Bad boy!"

Randy rolled the door shut behind him. The dog outside reared up on his hind legs and slammed against the side of the bus. Behind him, the old woman screeched and waved her hands and jumped up and down in the yard.

Randy crawled to the front seat, turned on the ignition, backed out of the driveway, and sped down the road with the black dog in full chase close behind. In the rearview mirror, the old woman ran behind the dog, flapping and waving her hands in a whirlwind of gravel-road dust.

Several days after he brought the Chow to Dr. Ed's clinic, Randy went back to the old woman's yard to watch the pack in the woods. While at least a dozen dogs loitered behind the house, shifted restlessly in the undergrowth, and stalked back and forth between the trees, the black dog had disappeared.

"Don't know where he went," the old woman said as she glared at the bridge with suspicion. "Just when you kind of get to know one, then they up and go away, or something. I pray for them, every night when I hear the noise, but . . ."

"What noise?"

"I don't know. Never mind."

"Was he aggressive toward you?"

"Who?"

"The black dog."

"Oh, no, never, ever. He adopted this yard kind of, and he was just ornery, you know, and they have every right to be, after what goes on 'round here." The old woman looked down the road as if searching for witnesses. Then she shook her head.

As Randy watched the pack from the old woman's yard, he tried to identify an alpha. It was a strange group, though, and there didn't seem to be much social structure. No one dog towered physically or psychologically over the rest, and without any hierarchical parameters, the skirmishes and the quick growls and snaps between them, never ended.

While a few looked as if they might have been on the streets a long time, the lack of any apparent hierarchy suggested that most of them were probably stray pets. Or whatever their owners considered them. All of the dogs were large, and all of them were thin. Those with short coats showed scars. Most of them had butchered ear crops, chopped tails, numerous abscesses, and puncture wounds around their heads, throats, and legs.

He went back for the next two weeks, but he never got close to any of the dogs, and while they didn't seem feral like those in the warehouse pack, they watched him from a distance with guarded eyes and trotted down the tracks when he got too near.

One day, the old woman called Randy at his grooming shop with her voice pitched toward panic.

"I got him. I got him. I got him trapped in my car."

"Who?"

"He's in my car. He's in my car. I got him in there with food."

"Who?"

"Who else? The ornery one. He's in my car, only . . ."

"Only what?"

"Only, he ain't so ornery right now."

JACK SMITH VS. FLOYD BOUDREAUX. The black gets the first hold as Bozo gets skin hold in throat. Black is getting into the throat of Bozo as Bozo works the ear trying for a shoulder. 50 to 25 bets being made. Bozo the favorite. Black is showing good and working for Bozo's throat. Black gets in Bozo's throat at 14, then Bozo throws one leg over the black's shoulder, gets an ear and throws the black dog. . . . The black acts as though he has shot his wad. Bozo has opened up the black's front leg and the black is weakening. . . . Bozo gets nape of neck and the black goes down. . . . The winner is declared in one hour and one minute.

So ended another "classic," as recorded in the "Vintage Match Report" by the *Pit Bull Reporter*.

Organized dogfighting is a felony in forty-three states, according to the Humane Society of the United States, and transporting dogs across state lines for participation in the sport violates the federal Animal Welfare Act. But combating the practice has proven about as successful as the government's war on drugs, and an estimated 40,000 Americans now take part in some aspect of the sport annually. Almost half of the human fatalities caused by dogs and investigated by the Humane Society of the United States in the past several years were related to Pit Bulls used for dogfighting.

Like any underground industry, dogfighting flourishes in impoverished, isolated areas where law enforcement, animal control, educational resources, and social philanthropy focus more on sheer survival than on the lack of healthier hobbies. So in addition to dogfighting's popularity in the backwoods pastures and empty barns of economically ruined rural communities, the breeders, trainers, and spectators who support dogfights increasingly congregate in the abandoned buildings and secluded fields of the declining inner city.

Part of the lure is money. "You can make money for real," says one eighteen-year-old, currently in jail for unrelated charges, who claims that teenagers in his St. Louis neighborhood treat a dogfight like a game of marbles.

"You fight 'em for, you know, street rights and for money, stuff like that. People raise them just to fight, you know what I'm sayin', they raise 'em mean by shoving red pepper up their nose, for real, you know, and feed 'em red meat with gunpowder, you know what I'm sayin'?"

According to another young man, who also asked not to be named, teenagers often buy fighting dogs from neighborhood breeders and then stash them in abandoned houses to keep them out of parental sight. "You know, the older people don't want no mean dog in the house and they're against the fighting anyways. But it goes on all the time."

When asked if many of the stray dogs in his neighborhood were fighting dogs, the young man shrugged. "You can't keep the dogs in those empty houses forever, you know what I'm sayin'? And if they don't fight good, then they get either killed or they run around loose like that."

Besides a lot of dead dogs, this practice produces an increasing number of aggressive strays, neither spayed nor neutered, who have been bred and trained for combat. When they aren't successful in the pit, they're dumped, half-dead already, into garbage cans, empty fields, rivers, abandoned buildings, basements, and closets. As Sgt.

Steve Brownstein, a Chicago police officer who specializes fighting cases, told the *Chicago Sun-Times* in 2000: "I've fighters tell me that, including teenagers, they're angry at a dog if it loses a fight, they want it to suffer, that's why they leave it locked in a closet to die a slow death of its injuries."

"Bait dogs" also make up a good portion of the urban stray population. Bait dogs are the smaller, weaker animals used to train the fighters; they are marked by missing limbs, numerous scars from the attacks, the wires by which they were tied down, wires now embedded in their legs, and by their conditioned fear of other dogs and humans.

Between 1999 and 2000, the number of 911 calls about animal abuse tripled in Chicago, and local shelters in Santa Clara and San Mateo Counties, in California, euthanized more than 1,250 Pit Bulls in 1999. The Pits made up almost 60 percent of the stray dogs brought in. In West Palm Beach, Florida, in the summer of 2000, sixty people were arrested, twelve dogs impounded, and $89,000 in cash and drugs was confiscated after a dogfighting ring was exposed. According to Palm Beach County Animal Care and Control, the stakes at the fights ranged from $5,000 to $10,000.

In 1998, Memphis animal control workers confiscated twenty-eight Pit Bulls used by a dogfighting ring. In August 2000, another thirty fighting Pit Bulls were found, and in October 2000 more than two dozen dogs were found chained in a muddy yard next to the decaying bodies of other dogs used for fighting. The following month, another dogfighting ring was broken up, and twenty-one dogs were confiscated. The month after that, twelve additional fighting dogs were seized.

Currently, most dogs confiscated because they were used for fighting are Pit Bulls. In 1999, according to the American Society for the Prevention to Cruelty to Animals, shelters in the following cities reported the highest number of Pit Bulls: New York, 7,285;

Chicago, 5,000; Boston, 4,535; Phoenix, 4,162; Oahu, 3,488; Knoxville, 2,000; San Francisco, 1,500; and Baltimore, 1,154.

With promises of easy money to be made breeding and gambling, the Internet now supplies lush cover for the growing subterranean market. Many dozens of supply companies on the Web sell custombuilt treadmills, armor-plated harnesses, energy-boosting supplements, balms for "hard nights," and chains that could anchor small boats.

Breeding operations are especially lucrative; on the Web you can find such names as Dead Man Kennels, Short Fuse Bulldogs, Deathrow Kennels, Terminator Kennels, Hard Dawgs Kennels, No Fear Kennels, Meaty Boys Kennels, Armageddon Kennels, Silent But Violent Kennels, and Brother to Brother Kennels.

There are also dozens of online magazines devoted to sport fighting. Readers enter by clicking on frothing beer mugs or two dogs engaged in battle or American flags flapping in the wind. The sites feature articles such as "How to School Your Bulldog" and "Legal Protection for Pit Breed Owners!" and offer all sorts of tidbits about hiding scars, breeding mean bitches, or ordering T-shirts that show two fighting dogs under the words "Till Death Do Us Part."

In the *Pit Bull Reporter,* the "Rules of the Pit" are spelled out:

Either handler may demand that the opposing handler and his cornerman bare their arms to the elbows; also, the handler may taste his opponent's dog's water before or after the contest. . . . The dogs shall be washed at pit-side in warm water and some approved washing powders and then rinsed.

The referee shall now ask "Are both corners ready?" If so, "Cornermen, out of the pit. Face your dogs. Let go."

When released at the words "Let Go," the dog must start

across at his opponent. He may waver from direct line, fall down, crawl, drag or push himself across, so long as he makes a continued effort and does not hesitate or stop until he has reached out and touched his opponent.
    The live dog is the winner.

He didn't seem like the same dog. As Randy peered through the Dodge Dart's windows, smudged with white road dust and dog slobber, he lay stretched out on the ripped-vinyl backseat and raised his head heavily when Randy tapped on the glass. His spine jutted out of his back, his eyes were sunk deep into his skull, and his face was as cut up as if he'd run through a plate-glass window.

"My God, what happened to him?"

"Dunno. Just showed up here one day all bedraggled and skinny. Got him into the car with some food, poor thing."

Randy opened the car's front door, sat down inside, and looked back at the dog.

"Hey guy, what happened to you?"

The dog didn't move, even when the old woman peered in through the back window and tapped on the glass. "Hello, Mr. Dog."

Randy got out of the front seat and looked up at the bridge, then over to the dogs watching from the woods, then down to the old woman bent over at the window.

"They fight them," he said, "don't they?"

The old woman pulled back from the window and maneuvered her eyes as far from his as she could.

"Don't they?"

She nodded.

"Why don't you call the police?"

"Can't," she said, her eyes still searching for escape. "They's in on it too. They shoot the dogs; the police do, just for fun. I've *seen* 'em. Besides . . ." She looked down the road. "They said they'd burn my house down if I told anyone."

As she confessed what she couldn't bear the burden of knowing anymore, the old woman started crying.

"They fight 'em, somewhere down the road. I hear it all night long on the weekends. Drives me batty. I can't sleep, can't eat, can't even watch TV. Then they throw 'em in the river when they lose. Or they kill 'em. I find dead dogs all the time 'round here.

"They fight 'em right out on the street, too, most every night. They bring two dogs out there and bet money on which one's gonna win. See, if you have the meanest dog 'round here, that means you get to own that part of the street. So they fight 'em constantly, all the time, to see who gets to own part of the street. You wouldn't believe it, how those poor dogs look when they're done, just wouldn't believe it."

As she released her secret, Randy stared through the glass at the dog on the backseat. It wasn't that he was "bad"; his aggression toward Randy hadn't been an insult or a calculated plot. From the day he was born, his faithfulness to his pack was unyielding, was as important to his being as his blood, and everything about him— how he walked, where he slept, when he ate—flowed from his need to belong. All he ever wanted was the hum of a pack in his ears, so if his human pack taunted and beat him and seemed pleased when he lashed back, then the direction of his behavior lay before him like a well-worn path through the weeds.

Even if they starved him, it didn't matter, not the pain or the hunger or the fear. So he responded to their goading, did what they wanted him to do, and in the end, when they deserted him anyway, all he understood was that he needed to find a new pack. And with the old woman, he had. She was his new alpha, and her yard was his new territory, and he did what he thought he had to. To belong.

When he first saw Randy come out of the garage with the Chow in his arms, he pushed his ears forward and waved his tail high— signs of territorial aggression. If his aggression had been based on fear, he would have tucked his tail, arched his back, and flattened his ears against his head when he attacked. He did what he was taught to do, because this time, he wanted to stay.

"They use the little dogs to teach the big dogs how to fight. . . ."

The old woman's confession wasn't one he hadn't heard before. Dogfighting flourished throughout the city, and innocent people were often its secondhand victims—not only people like the old woman, but also the kids who grew up desensitized to seeing pain in other living creatures.

The golden Chow, the dogs in the woods, and the black dog curled up in the backseat weren't fighting dogs, not successful ones anyway. They were either discarded losers or leftover bait. He'd rescued a lot of dogs that had been used as bait: the starving, yellow Lab-Shepherd mix chained and mutilated in a yard where a healthy Pit Bull roamed free; puppies skinned alive near a crack house on the East Side; the terrier mix with ribbonlike scars up and down his front legs from the wire used to tie him down.

Randy opened the back door of the car. There were no growls or threatening poses, no lunges or displays of strength. Like most of the dogs he rescued, the black dog had given up.

"You gonna save him?"

"Yep."

"Think he'll be all right?"

"Yep."

The old woman nodded her head and looked out at the dogs in the trees.

"I figure they just get fed up with getting beaten all the time and find better company with themselves."

When the black dog was tucked safely in the back of the bus, Randy pulled out his cell phone and dialed Dr. Ed.

"I'm on my way in with an injured one," Randy said. "He's beaten up pretty bad."

He looked in the rearview mirror at the old woman standing in the yard, waving and watching him leave.

"The usual," he said into the phone.

Chapter Six

When Skies Are Gray

Compton, Midnight, and Taz sat at the side of the warehouse and watched Randy finger the bottom of his shirt as he stood and stared into the three Quonset huts.

The corrugated structures looked like immense tin drums sliced in half lengthwise and laid out flat on the ground. Their front and back doors were missing, and while they were large enough for a semi truck to pass through, the interiors of the buildings were so dark that looking in was like looking into the hereafter.

A commuter train skimmed the northern horizon, and a flock of crows swerved around a nearby utility tower. Like red-tailed hawks and small falcons, the crows thrived on trash-strewn urban pastures. As the whine of the train faded to the east, Randy cleared his throat.

"Sunshine?"

The pregnant yellow dog had disappeared from the pack several weeks before. Though Randy had searched the wide-open savanna of weeds and utility towers behind the Quonset huts and walked the tracks for miles calling her name, he had found nothing but flattened pennies and wine jugs. He had vetoed a large search party of Stray Rescue volunteers, because if Sunshine was still alive, the unfamiliar scents and voices would only drive her deeper into seclusion.

Because street dogs often travel miles on any given day, Randy crisscrossed a seven-block perimeter around the warehouse, shouting Sunshine's name over the mufflerless clamor of the bus. The only people he ever encountered were the men pushing their shopping carts of aluminum to Can Man Recycling up Chouteau, and when he asked them if they'd seen a skinny yellow dog running around, they waved him away with toothless laughs.

Randy drove to every area within five miles where he knew other packs ran, hoping she had joined up with one of them. He searched every abandoned house, tramped through every empty field, called every shelter in the city. Then, every evening, when he went back to the warehouse and waited for the rest of the pack to return from its day, he hoped to see Sunshine lagging behind. But they always came home without her, and he knew, as he knew that the sun would soon set and the lights of downtown would go up and the squeaking of the shopping carts would cease with the oncoming night, that Sunshine, or her body, was in one of the Quonset huts. And he couldn't make himself go in.

"I mean, *look* at them," he said. Compton, Midnight, and Taz sat by the side of the warehouse and bit at small, spring-hatched flies. "Anything could be in there."

Bats, murder victims, a secret leper colony for all he or the health department knew. Headless horsemen, spies in hiding, genetically altered man-eating ants. He paced back and forth in front of the three caverns like a losing coach on the sidelines. Short of licking plague germs off a public toilet seat, nothing appealed to him less than venturing into the buildings' limitless corruption.

As if to initiate some action, Taz woofed once in Randy's direction, and, uncomfortable in the line of their questioning stares,

Randy nodded his head at the three dogs, turned back to the middle Quonset hut, and cleared his throat again.

"Sun-shine!"

The interior swallowed Randy's voice, churned it around, and spat it back out, along with a fleet of startled pigeons who exploded through the door with a clatter.

Randy froze, gasped, recoiled sideways, and fell backward into the weeds. Compton, Midnight, and Taz stood up. They cocked their heads and stared at the air that Randy seconds before had inhabited. Taz stepped forward and woofed.

Randy pulled himself up from the ground and waved in the direction of the dogs.

"Don't be scared," he called across the tops of the weeds. "Just some pigeons."

The next morning a cigarette dangled from Randy's mouth as he clomped through heavy mud on the west end of the three Quonset huts. An early spring rain had fallen the night before, and as he walked, lids at half-mast against the spiraling cigarette smoke, he searched the soggy ground for paw prints.

"In the winter, when it snows, it's a lot easier to see where they've been," he said. "I can follow the tracks of this pack for miles when it snows, because there aren't any people or cars or anything to mess them up.

"They pretty much follow the same routine every day," he said as he rounded the corner at the back of the last Quonset hut. "By late morning, they're usually out in the yard in front of the warehouse waiting for me. I feed them, and they stay in the warehouse as long as I'm there. When I leave, they take off along the tracks going west, out toward the truck yards and empty factories. Then they come back to the warehouse at dusk." One of Randy's volunteers helped him drop food at the warehouse several days a week, in part to get the dogs used to other humans and in part to give Randy more time to search for Sunshine.

Later that morning, as he sat with the pack inside the warehouse and listened to the volatile weather bang loose sheets of metal against the roof, Katlin stood up from her resting spot next to Midnight and ambled closer to Randy. Midnight watched her through bored half-closed eyes, but Compton, conscious of any shift in the pack's physical or mental status, stayed alert in his corner.

Space was important to them; it was a way of measuring rank. When they rested, Compton's space was big, and no one else went near him, while Katlin's space was small since she ranked lowest now that Sunshine was gone.

Randy sat on the tire rim and drew jagged designs with the end of the snare in ashes still smoldering from a fire the night before.

"Can you imagine having to keep warm with a fire like this? If I were stuck out in the cold, even if I was freezing to death, I wouldn't have a clue how to build one."

The tip of the snare found an ember and Randy flipped it into the air. "When I was kid, I used to plan ways to escape my father and go live in the woods. I was going to learn how to build fires and hunt food, you know, live like Robert Redford did in that movie in the mountains, befriending squirrels and wolves, eating tree bark, with no people around to hurt you. . . ."

Randy shoved the snare in and out of a pocket of ashes. Katlin sighed, dropped her head onto her outstretched legs, and watched him from the tops of her eyes.

"I should have set a trap for Sunshine," he said as the snare went deep, and stray smoke drifted up from the bottom. He flipped more ashes out of the pile, and Katlin jumped back toward Midnight.

"I know she's probably dead, but I wake up every morning and think that maybe today I'll find her. You know? I think that maybe she's not dead yet. Maybe she's just hurt, or maybe she's nursing her pups in some secret place I haven't found yet, and if I just look hard enough, maybe I'll find her in time."

Compton sat in the corner as his amber eyes patrolled the group on the warehouse floor, slow and officious, like a lifeguard watching an almost-empty beach. Sunny bit at the fleas on her forelegs. Midnight and Katlin closed their eyes. Taz lay in his usual post by the open door and flicked his eyes from the Quonset huts, to the yard, to Randy, to Compton, and back to the Quonset huts again.

"He stares out at those things like he knows someone's in there," Randy said. He shuddered.

"Any time I bring volunteers out here, they always seem so concerned about the guy who lives here. But I could care less. I know it's bad, but he—or whoever it is that lives here—scares me, and I wish he'd just go away."

Randy stood up, reached into a back pocket, and pulled out his wallet.

"I leave him money sometimes, though." He fished out a twenty and anchored it under the edge of the tire rim. "Maybe he'll be good to the dogs."

The rain continued for the next several days. By the time the weather cleared, a black, oily pool had formed in Randy's normal pacing zone in front of the Quonset huts. He took it as a sign: he'd have to go in.

He squared his shoulders and pushed heavy canvas bite gloves onto his hands. "I'm going to walk around the edge of the water and go in."

He zipped up his jacket and looked back across the water. "I'm just going to walk right in."

He tugged down the rim of his baseball cap, then dipped into his pocket and pulled out his cigarettes. "I'm going to light this cigarette and go in."

He lit the cigarette and put the pack back into his pocket. Then he took the gloves off and put them back in his pocket too. Then he tugged down on the baseball cap again. Then he puffed out his cheeks.

"I'm going in."

The pond was only the size of a backyard swimming pool, but with the cigarette dangling from his lips and the snare held out in front of him like a dagger, it took Randy twenty minutes to walk around it to the first Quonset hut's door.

Cold air blew from the black interior like wind rushing out of a cave. Randy cleared his throat and leaned forward from the waist and steadied his snare before him. He cleared his throat again.

"Sunshine?"

Pigeons rustled deep inside. Randy winced. "It's like a frickin' mausoleum," he whispered.

Randy stepped closer to the door. He leaned forward from his waist again, and squinted into the cold, musty darkness.

"I can't see anything."

The pigeons quieted.

"Hello? Excuse me, hello?"

Wings whirled inside.

"Hello? Excuse me, I'm, um, coming in now."

More pigeons murmured and whirled.

"Excuse me, uh, I'm—"

"I bet you were *born* in a frickin' mausoleum!"

Randy's eyes rounded as he stared into the talking abyss.

"Weren't you?" the voice demanded from the pit.

Randy shook his head and dropped the snare.

"*Weren't you*? And if you touch my stuff, Coyote Man, I swear to God, I'll put you in one! You hear me, Coyote Man? You hear me?"

But Randy didn't hear. Before the last, raspy syllable cleared the doorway, he was two-thirds of the way to the bus.

In the late 1960s, Dr. Michael Fox, an animal behavior researcher and associate professor of psychology at Washington University, St. Louis, wanted to see whether it was instinct or training that enabled wild dogs to hunt prey. A group of individually raised coyote pups and beagle puppies were tested at eight weeks of age for their reactions toward a young laboratory rat.

The coyote pups were recorded as doing some of the following when face-to-face with the rat: "Immediate grab-bite-carry, then crush bite . . . crushes head . . . eats off hind leg, then tail . . . rips off skin . . . eats intestines . . . removes and eats head."

The Beagle pups, however, didn't have a clue: "Wags tail . . . sniffs . . . licks rat's face . . . play solicits . . . barks at rat . . . leaps, leaps, leaps . . . plays with tail of rat . . . sustained playful interaction for last five minutes. Rat is alive and well."

Fox also studied a pack of feral dogs over the course of one summer and never once saw them catch a squirrel, rat, or cat, despite all the chasing they did. Owing to domestication and selective breeding, he concluded, the dogs no longer knew how to act like wild animals.

Much of the problem—from a stray dog's perspective—is that the wolves who became members of human packs thousands of years ago evolved differently from those who stayed in the wild. The result of this genetic divergence is a full-grown canine who looks and acts like a wolf puppy.

Behaviorally, dogs act like juvenile wolves when, for example, they greet their owners with licking and jumping, which is a wolf pup's way of urging its elders to regurgitate food. The tracks of adult wolves usually run in a straight line, direct and focused in their goal, while the tracks of wolf pups and domesticated dogs meander as if they're not sure where they're headed. Dogs and wolf pups whine for attention; adult wolves, for the most part, don't. In fact, one of the few occasions on which adult wolves bark is when they're engaged in a fight for dominance and the outcome still isn't clear. This leads some researchers to wonder whether adult wolf barking—and that of domesticated dogs—is a sign of indecision.

Dogs have smaller bodies, snouts, and teeth, and their brains are 20 percent smaller than those of wolves. Dogs' ears also usually drop, whereas wolves' ears prick up in adulthood.

In a wolf pack, females mature sexually at two years and then come into heat once a year. Usually only the alpha female and one or two higher-ranking males mate, and they produce small litters, which are then cared for by the entire pack, with both males and females regurgitating food for the cubs.

A female dog, on the other hand, reaches puberty between six and twelve months of age; if she isn't spayed, she comes into heat every six or seven months and produces litters of between six and ten puppies. Male dogs produce sperm year-round and are therefore fertile throughout the year, while most wild canids studied only produce sperm during the breeding season.

Many researchers believe that the physical differences between wolves and dogs did not arise through conscious human direction. Rather, as the "tamer" wolves became more and more dependent on the human packs they followed for food, and as their more "docile" genes were passed on to evolving generations of offspring, the genetic behavioral changes trapped adult dogs in wolf puppy clothing.

In the 1960s and 1970s, the Russian geneticist D. K. Belyaev wanted to breed tameness into silver foxes so they would be more suitable for fur ranching. After selecting and breeding the tamest foxes (those least aggressive and afraid of humans) over twelve years, he produced foxes that very much resembled domesticated dogs: they became sexually mature early in life and went into heat more than once a year; they had curled tails and floppy ears; and they retained into adulthood many of the juvenile behavior patterns of wild canids, including tail wagging, licking, and face sniffing.

According to the biologist Raymond Coppinger, tameness is exhibited by wild juvenile canids, but not by adults. When the "tame" genes were passed on from generation to generation, so were many of the other characteristics of young animals. In the normal life cycle of a wild canid, silver foxes, like domesticated dogs, arrested in puppyhood. As a result, they look to their superiors for care, they're noisy, they socialize with animals of other species, and they are not particularly adept at forming working packs or raising puppies in the wild.

Domesticated dogs are neotenic, which means that they retain the charm and innocence of young animals and are docile, submissive, and forever "immature."

Randy wandered through the dirty gray silence of the warehouse, swishing a new snare in the dirt. The pigeons cooed in the rafters.

"I should have trapped her," he said. "I misjudged my ability to get her to trust me, and now she's gone. But I'm going to trap the rest of them, I swear I will. I don't care how psychologically messed up it makes them. I don't care if they never get adopted out. I'll keep them in my basement if I have to, and I don't care what Paul or the Homeowners Association or the Department of Agriculture says about it."

He shuffled to the open door, squinted against the afternoon light, and cupped his hands around his mouth.

"Sunshine!"

Pigeons flapped above him and a distant siren wailed.

"Sunshine!"

Randy eyed the three Quonset huts across the yard. Self-loathing flooded his face. He shook his head.

"I have to go in there."

He reached into his coat pocket, popped open the bottle of Xanax prescribed by his psychiatrist to quell panic attacks, and let two small white pills tumble into his palm. Into his hand, he muttered: "Not going to let some old homeless guy scare me . . . not a victim . . . have every right . . . choose to be afraid."

Without any more mental preparation than throwing the two pills into his mouth, Randy marched across the yard to the Quonset huts, a robot stiff on autopilot.

He charged the first structure without pausing and disappeared behind its inky veil.

"Sunshine!"

The word ricocheted off the corrugated interior and pigeons convulsed all around him. Outside light filtered in from both ends of the building but dimmed to darkness in between.

Randy kept on walking. He walked straight through.

"Sunshine!"

He marched the length of the empty building, dark and cool and littered with dead leaves, and when he reached the open door at the back end, he stomped through, veered right, and headed into the middle building.

It, too, was empty, but he walked its length anyway, calling Sunshine's name. By the time he emerged through its front door, the Xanax kicked in, and he pivoted left, without stopping, toward the homeless man's domain.

"I'm coming in," he called as he scooped up the snare he'd dropped the day before.

As in the other two huts, light from the ends of the building petered out in the middle. In the muted shadows off center, an empty sleeping bag stretched out on a gnawed, yellowed mattress with stuffed plastic garbage bags at its head. Around the bed, clothes hung from the corners of cardboard boxes and on metal poles balanced against the walls. Newspapers and books and plastic dishes stood stacked against the opposite wall, which was chalk-scribbled with complex trigonometric functions.

"Hello?" Randy's eyes searched for the building's occupant. "Sunshine?"

But, like the others, the Quonset hut was vacant.

Later, Randy slumped passed the warehouse toward the bus parked on Chouteau, as one of his volunteers, Dawn, pulled her car into the yard. Randy nodded to her, but her eyes shifted from Randy's face to the warehouse door behind him.

"Who's that?" she asked.

"Huh?" Randy swiveled toward the warehouse.

Sunshine sat in the door with late-afternoon light collecting around her yellow fur like a halo. Randy tripped toward the door.

Sunshine cocked her head as he ran toward her, then stood up and backed into the darkness of the warehouse. Randy stopped just outside the doorway and crouched down as he caught his breath.

"Sunshine, where *were* you?"

She sat down and swished her tail back and forth on the dirt, then turned and hobbled deeper into the building. She hadn't had that limp before. She'd also lost her belly, and her nipples were dark and dried-up instead of a newly suckled pink: she wasn't nursing any pups.

When she reached the deep gloom inside, she turned her head back to see if Randy followed.

"Hey girl, what happened to your leg? Where's the rest of the gang?"

Randy tiptoed into the building and looked for the rest of the pack. But Sunshine was alone, and instead of flitting away as she usually did when he got too near, she circled and lay down on the dirt.

"Things are bad, aren't they, girl?"

When she looked up into his eyes, Randy saw the look he'd seen before in hundreds of dogs when they realized that being wild was over, when they realized they couldn't hunt, couldn't fight disease, couldn't depend on the pack. It was a look that said they were tired, a look that said they had no choices anymore. On Sunshine, who had probably watched her pups die slowly one by one, probably licked them and nudged them and savored the warmth of their bodies until the awful moment of cold clarity hit her, it was a look that said, *I give up.*

Feral dogs like Sunshine accepted Randy as their leader only when their desperation got so deep that there was no room for the suspicions that had clawed at them from birth. They hadn't grown up in a human pack and didn't understand that it was a safe place to be, so they'd join only if they already trusted Randy. Once that happened, they turned over their imagined independence like what it was—a useless, worn-out dream.

Randy walked the short distance between them, not bothering to hide the snare. Behind him, Dawn stood in the doorway.

"What's going on, girl? You ready to come home with me?"

Randy talked in a monotone, so she wouldn't sense his own rising fear. He'd only have one chance to get the snare around her neck; if she bolted and the loop didn't hold, the trauma would shatter the fragile trust he'd built, and he'd probably never see her again.

Sunshine cocked her head as she watched him approach. When he got down on his knees, the change in posture worried her, and she stood up, slowly, as if every bone in her delicate body harbored pain.

"I know how scared you are."

Sunshine's eyes darted back and forth between his face and the snare in his hand. She seemed to sense the change in him, seemed to smell his anxiety like her own. And she knew anxiety well, having been afraid her whole life.

"You'll be safe with me."

She also knew pain. She'd lost her pack. She'd lost her pups. There were no warm bodies around her anymore.

"I know how horrible it must have been."

Randy inched closer and extended his hand, as if reaching for someone on the edge of a cliff.

"None of this is your fault. None of it."

He moved his fingers toward her forehead. If he could just touch her once, if she could just feel the warmth of his fingers on her fur, she'd disconnect from the emotional force field around her and give in. And that's what happened in the end, giving in. The transition was never easy; Sunshine might glue her devotion to just one human being for the rest of her life. But with the right attention and training, she might learn to have faith in one, then another, then another, until her belief in the human pack reached full-blown loyalty. Either way, once she realigned her trust, she would make a more devoted companion than a dog who'd never been so alone. She might not ever learn to fetch a ball or sit on command, and she might always carry the physical and emotional scars, but until the last breath left her body, she would always remain more grateful.

"You're just scared of the unknown."

He leaned closer.

"But the unknown . . ."

He reached forward.

". . . is a great place to be."

Then he touched her. She felt a human hand, probably for the first time in her life, and Randy hummed as he ran his fingers across her silky fur.

She didn't move. Didn't flinch. Didn't bolt. Didn't bite.

"You make me haaa-peee . . ."

She just closed her eyes.

And exhaled deeply.

Midnight and Sunshine in front of the Quonset huts

Randy and Katlin in warehouse

Randy watches Katlin and Midnight in warehouse.

Junkyard pups

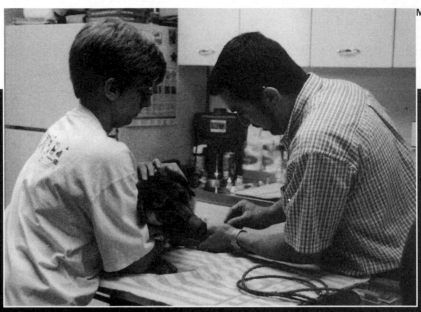

Dr. Ed Migneco attends to the junkyard mother after her rescue.

Pack of strays

Two strays, Sundance and Cassidy, approach food thrown by Randy.

Sundance approaches Randy.

M.

The pair is starving. The rescue is easy.

Sundance and Cassidy on the way home in the bus after the rescue

M. F

Part Two

Chapter Seven

Left Behind

Mary Zorich pulled out her wallet and watched Dr. Ed Migneco add up the bill. At her feet, her two mixed-breed dogs, Daisy and Kiko, looked up at a calico cat who sat on the counter and stared back with lazy, slit-eyed defiance.

"Lots of Stray Rescue dogs here today," Dr. Ed said, without looking up.

Mary shifted from one foot to the other and searched the walls for diversions. Diplomas, awards, certificates, the life cycle of heartworm, a bulletin board plastered with overlapping photos of Stray Rescue success stories.

"Really." She ironed out the word as flat as she could.

Dr. Ed nodded and hunched deeper over the bill, and Mary hustled her gaze from the photos to a special certification in canine and feline practice from the American Board of Veterinary Practitioners and focused on that instead. She knew where this was going, knew it like the chorus of a childhood song.

"You going to foster one?" Dr. Ed asked.

Mary shook her head so hard she felt her red hair slap the sides of her face. In the past several years, she'd fostered more dogs for

Randy than she could count, and while she loved and still thought about every one, she was coming down from fifteen years in the corporate world and had her own mental healing to think about.

"No."

No more dogs. No more haunted animals who cried in their sleep, urinated from fear, and circled in the corner of her living room for hours as if trying to get away from themselves. No more dogs who gnawed from frustration at their own skin or snapped at the air when there was nothing around. No more cringing or pacing or fear biting or wailing. No more dogs right now. Especially not after Mia.

Janet Carp, the Stray Rescue volunteer who had helped Randy during Bonnie's labor, found the two-year-old brown-spotted street mix in a junkyard raising three puppies on her own. After Randy and Janet staged a weeklong rescue, Mia and one of her puppies went to Mary's for fostering.

It took five days before Mia let Mary approach her, and even then she cringed at the touch of Mary's hand. As for Missy, the puppy, she was totally feral. She hid under anything bigger than she was and stared off into space and shook.

Mary focused her attention first on the puppy, Missy: being so young, she was more susceptible to the lure of a new pack. Mary spent hours on the floor and talked and sang and threw food to the wild, untouched thing under her couch while Mia clung to bad experience and shuddered in her own corner.

At night Mary ushered Mia and Missy into her bedroom along with Daisy and Kiko to reconstruct the security of a pack in a den. During the day, before she left the house, Mary scattered her clothes on the floor, so her scent stayed fixed in their minds. Within three weeks, Missy realized that Mary—not Mia—was her only source of food, and thus her new alpha, and she eventually crawled out of her solitary shadows and surrendered to her need to belong. She gave in to human touch and human play and human scent all around her. When she ate, she ate from human hands; when she was left behind on the floor, she crouched and jumped and yapped at the air and begged to be in human arms. She played with the other dogs now, too, because they, unlike her mother, were part of her new pack.

From her corner, Mia watched. She watched like something trapped, like something held at the border between one world and another, unable to get across, and as her puppy loped ahead with little trouble at all, Mia sat shackled to her fear. She sat and watched for weeks.

One night, as Mary and Missy sat on the couch and watched TV, Kiko and Daisy asleep at their feet, Mia made her move. She padded across the room as if negotiating a plain of thin ice. Mary watched her from the corner of her eye as Mia sniffed first toward Kiko and Daisy on the floor, then toward Missy and Mary. Then, with the delicacy of someone asking for a favor, she laid her nose on the couch.

Mary looked over at Mia. Mia's eyes rolled away, but her nose stayed put. Mary edged her hand across the couch until she felt warm puffs of air from Mia's nostrils and then walked her fingers up Mia's nose until they rested between her ears. Then she scratched behind Mia's forehead and Mia, eyes closed, leaned into her hand.

No. No more dogs. It took too much time, too much energy, too much patience to foster a dog. And it hurt too much to give them everything she had and then, because they were fosters, give them away.

"No," she said out loud.

Dr. Ed's eyes scrolled the bill. He scribbled down a total, slid it across the counter, and shrugged.

"Then you better not go into the back and look at the dog in the last cage."

Two weeks before, Dr. Ed had stood in an alley behind the bald yard of an abandoned house and slipped Acepromazine into some food. Across the hard-packed dirt, two mixed-breed dogs sniffed the air. They were males, both limping and thin. The smaller one had short black hair, but the other, with an infection that sealed one eye shut, was so covered in mange, Dr. Ed couldn't tell what color he was.

They clung to the shadow of the abandoned house. While they showed no signs of aggression, they were skittish, and skittish dogs made the worst biters. Because they'd never seen him before, Dr. Ed knew they might not eat the food if he put it on the ground, so he handed it to Ellie Harris, a Stray Rescue volunteer who'd been feeding them for months.

"How long will it take, Dr. Ed?" she asked as they backed out of the yard toward the open door of Randy's bus.

"Not long."

He didn't like giving sedatives to street dogs like this, because he never knew how they'd react. He had to guess their weight and their health histories, had to take chances he didn't like to take. He'd been in veterinary practice for almost two decades, and while he understood that there were vast tracts of unexplored terrain and that he sometimes had to feel along in the dark, not knowing the way always caught him off guard and ate at his professional confidence. Still, bad weather was coming, and it was time to get these two off the streets.

Dr. Ed and Ellie crawled into the bus and waited with Randy as the two dogs crawled low to the ground toward the food.

"Go on, eat it," Ellie whispered.

The people who lived next door to the abandoned house had told Ellie that the dogs' owners had moved away and left them behind long ago. The dogs had stayed in the house waiting for them to return, but by the time Ellie found them, they were starving and skittish and ravaged by mange, still waiting for someone to come home. She named the large dog Penn and the small black one Sota.

"Go on," she whispered again.

Behind the two dogs, moss and wild ivy crawled across the back of the crumbling brick bungalow. Its windows were broken: a sign of vacancy. Intact windows meant people inhabited the house; broken windows meant that dogs lived inside.

Some medical researchers use the "broken windows" index to predict gonorrhea rates in a given neighborhood. Wherever there is substandard housing, they reason, there is probably also inadequate education and health care services, so sexually transmitted diseases and infant mortality run wild.

In this neighborhood on the south side of the city, every second building had broken-out windows, fewer than two-thirds of the women over seventeen had a high school diploma, and the infant mortality rate soared, almost 132 percent of the national average.

If babies survived their first year here, legions of other threats lined up on well-mapped coordinates to greet them: malnutrition, lead poisoning, physical abuse, diabetes, drugs, HIV, fires, gang warfare, heart failure, kidney failure, and asthma. Every year in the city of St. Louis alone, forty people die from asthma and another three thousand are hospitalized—four times the rate of the surrounding suburbs. Most of the asthmatics are young and come from low-income neighborhoods where old overcrowded houses, cockroaches, factories, rodents, highways, and open, abandoned lots belch smoke, pollen, smog, dust, and mold into their lungs.

Stray bullets, stray pathogens, stray dogs. In addition to everything else, the list of diseases a child in a neighborhood like this could catch from the glut of stray dogs was enough to make Dr. Ed want to hide—ticks, roundworm, hookworm, tapeworm, ringworm, sarcoptic mange. They could catch Lyme disease or leptospirosis or fleas. And none of those came close to what would happen if any of the dogs contracted rabies.

During the time that America grew into the scientific and industrial wonder of the world, the incidence of rabies in humans plummeted, a marker of the country's social evolution. But in 1999, more than 7,000 animal cases of rabies were reported. Ninety-two percent of these were reported in wild animals, mostly raccoons and bats, but the number of raccoons and bats living in deserted, trash-strewn city areas is on the increase, as is the number of unvaccinated stray dogs who come into contact with them. These days the threat of rabies isn't so foreign. Every year, about 18,000 Americans get rabies shots after exposure to wild animals that may have been rabid; and the two starving male dogs in the yard gulping down Dr. Ed's food were just about as wild as any raccoon or skunk or bat.

"Will it knock them totally out?" Randy asked from behind the wheel.

Dr. Ed shook his head. "It's a pre-anesthetic sedative. It'll just make them sleepy."

But what calmed a fairly healthy animal in the safety of his clinic could produce any number of unexpected effects on dogs like these. For one thing, they were keyed up; the adrenaline surging through their veins might dilute or override the sedative. What worried him more was that they might ingest the sedative and then bolt before it took effect; in that case, they might fall asleep anywhere and become vulnerable to all sorts of danger—cars, bored teenagers, people looking for fighting-dog bait. He hated not knowing.

Dr. Ed had grown up in a working-class Italian neighborhood on the south side of the city. He couldn't remember a time when he didn't want to know *more*. He wanted to know more about the small animals his father, a local high school principal, brought home during summer breaks. He wanted to know more about why birds flew and frogs hopped and guinea pigs ate like small cows. He wanted to know more about the dogs and cats brought into the local vet clinic where he worked part-time during high school—how they got sick, how they got well, how they sometimes died—and about what the vet could do when they were in pain. Animals and medicine were unending journals, and the potential of a lifelong subscription buoyed him all the way through vet school.

Even six years after he graduated from the University of Missouri and took over the local vet's practice in his South Side neighborhood, Dr. Ed needed to know more. So he spent two grueling years studying for special certification by the American Board of Veterinary Practitioners. He had earned the title of diplomate, which meant he was a board-certified specialist in small animal practice. After that, he spent fifty hours a year in continuing education. He didn't want to miss the next case just because he hadn't attended a seminar where he might have learned more about it.

But none of the classes, the seminars, or the book work taught Dr. Ed anything about days like this.

Penn and Sota showed no signs of dropping. They paced the yard like sentries, shooting nervous glances at the open side door of the bus. Unlike the dogs in the warehouse pack, who had colonized large stretches of uninhabited territory and focused mainly on finding food, Penn and Sota shared a neighborhood with human beings; they had to watch out for cars, bikes, chains, rocks, bullets, and bricks in addition to scrounging up something to eat. They were inexperienced brothers-in-arms, adolescents defending the homestead while waiting for their "parents" to return, and while they claimed the house as their territory, all they did to defend it was pace back and forth in the yard. They didn't know what else to do.

"How much longer?" Randy asked.

Dr. Ed shrugged and checked his watch like someone waiting for a late train. "We might as well get out there. I don't want them dropping in a place where we can't find them."

Randy and Dr. Ed grabbed snare poles and bite gloves and jumped out of the bus with Ellie behind them. The dogs stopped pacing and watched them fan out along the back of the yard.

Penn's ears pricked forward. Sota crouched low to the ground. Then they bolted, full throttle, over the back fence and out into the alley, where they raced down the cobblestones side by side and disappeared through a hole under the porch of another house.

Dr. Ed and Randy followed. They jumped onto the porch above the hiding dogs, and as Randy dangled the snare's noose in front of the hole, the back door of the house swung open, and a woman stood there, staring out. Randy yanked up the snare and shoved it behind his back, as if he'd been caught shoplifting.

"We're, uh, trying to catch some dogs."

The woman grunted and slammed the door back shut.

Randy lowered the noose again. When the top of Sota's head popped out and into the wide-open loop, Randy yanked up on the lever and the noose snapped tight.

"Got him!"

With the snare tightening around his neck, Sota lunged forward and wrenched Randy off the porch behind him. He twisted and tugged and bucked like an unbroken horse on a lasso. Randy dropped to his knees and braced his arms as Sota snarled and whipped his head from side to side.

"Dr. Ed, *help.*"

The snare's pole snapped, and Sota dashed from the yard and out onto the street, the splintered pole clacking on the pavement behind him. In the meantime, Penn dashed out from under the porch, and Ellie followed him in the opposite direction down the street.

Sota headed back to the yard of the abandoned house he shared with Penn and bounded up the front steps and into an enclosed porch. When Dr. Ed and Randy reached the yard, Randy stopped, planted his gloved hands on his knees, and gulped in air.

"Gotta quit smoking," he gasped.

"Stay out here," Dr. Ed said. "I'll flush him out."

Dr. Ed sprung up onto the enclosed porch. It was risky, cornering a terror-stricken dog with drugs riding roughshod through his bloodstream, but every minute spent trying to catch a stray could be the animal's last chance.

When the vet stepped toward him, the small black dog cringed, crouched low, ears flat, as small as he could make himself against the side of the porch. Dr. Ed extended the catchpole's noose, and it hovered, a hoop between one world and another, over Sota's quivering head.

Outside, still bent over, Randy watched sweat drip down from his forehead and onto a faded lottery ticket plastered to the sidewalk. He turned his head to look for Ellie, but she and Penn were gone.

Up inside the porch, a rustle, a muffled bump, a series of scratches and scrapes. Then, at the door of the porch, the whites of Sota's eyes. Sota's neck stretched taut against the noose, and his front paws paddled air. Dr. Ed's pale hands clutched the end of the catchpole. Sota dove into the yard.

Randy sprang forward and grabbed the dog, who thrashed and twirled and clawed at the ground and spun and snapped his teeth in the air.

"It's okay, boy, it's okay."

The dog pitched a high-note yelp. He kicked his back legs. Randy grabbed him around the midsection and hugged him down to the ground.

"It's okay now. Everything's going to be okay."

Randy leaned down onto the small, writhing dog, who soon stilled and then moaned.

"Shhh. Shhh."

Randy felt Sota's shoulders and back relax and watched his nails pull out of the dirt. He ran his glove along the ridges of ribs, and scratched along the arc where Sota's back leg met his belly.

Dr. Ed pulled a syringe out of his pocket, yanked the cap off with his teeth, and plunged it into Sota's shoulder.

"Tranquilizer," Dr. Ed said as he stood up and studied the street. "Where's Ellie?"

Randy stared down at Sota's watery, infected eyes and shrugged. "Dunno."

"He'll be okay," Dr. Ed said.

Randy nodded. He picked Sota's weakening body from the ground and held him against his chest.

"Dr. Ed says you're going to be okay," he whispered. As he stood, he felt the familiar wet warmth of dog urine seep down the front of his shirt.

Ellie couldn't catch Penn that afternoon. She went back to the abandoned house every day for several months and watched him wander and sniff around the yard as if searching for something misplaced long ago.

"He was totally lost, being all alone without Sota," Ellie said.

While she dropped food for him, as she had before, he didn't eat much, and he no longer wagged his tail when he saw her coming. She tried trapping him again, but he had grown wise, and several months later, with the mange eating away at the last of his fur, he began staying with the two male dogs in another broken-windowed house down the street.

"He was never the same," Ellie said. "He didn't eat much, and he just wandered aimlessly up and down the street."

She had tried so hard to catch him that day with Randy and Dr. Ed—had run and run and run up and down the streets and through the alleys and across the fields and backyards, run until sweat rolled down her face, run until she couldn't breathe. It was like chasing something in a dream, where every step she pushed forward pulled Penn one step farther away.

Penn walked the streets for months looking for Sota, ate when he had to, slept the rest of the time. And then, when he was nearly bald from the mange, he disappeared from the street.

Ellie's voice edged toward an octave just below cracking.

"I never saw him again," she said.

Mary Zorich lay down sideways on the couch and let her red hair splash over Sota's black coat.

"So of course, I go back and look into the last cage," she said as she sat back up and Sota crawled into her lap. "And I see this, this dog with mange and heartworm, all scared and shivering in the corner, afraid for his life. So of course, I brought him home—much to the dismay of my husband and the Homeowners Association."

In the Zorichs' town house, nestled on a private court in Lafayette Square with a two-dog-per-home limit, chew toys for three dogs lay scattered across every wood floor and antique Turkish rug.

"For four days after I brought him home, he just sat in the corner and wouldn't eat or drink. He didn't have any bowel movements, and he only urinated when he was afraid. And he was afraid of everything. He was a lot like Mia. Every noise scared him. Even if I just took a spoon out of the kitchen drawer, he'd cringe and try to hide."

One day, when Mary said the word "sit," Sota sat. Once he'd been somebody's pet, but he'd been horribly abused, which was why he ran, she guessed, when she pulled out utensils from the drawer. They triggered memories of beatings.

The first morning when she left for work, Mary put Sota in a steel crate, but by the time she got home that night, Sota sat loose and shivering in his corner. He'd ripped the floor of the crate and then rolled it up like a tube of toothpaste.

"And he did it with his molars," she said as she pulled Sota's top and bottom lips apart to expose teeth ground down to the gums. "See? He has no teeth. Most dogs who've been on the streets a long time don't have front or bottom teeth, because they use them to rip tin cans and things open."

Mary let Sota run loose during the day. Dogs don't soil their dens if they can help it, so a lot of stray dogs who have lived in abandoned houses are completely house-trained. This was the case with Sota.

After a few days, Sota followed Mary's other two dogs, Daisy and Kiko, into the kitchen, then up the stairs to the bedroom, then out the back door onto the porch. When he finally started to eat, Mary took him outside on the leash.

"I nicknamed him Rat Boy, because he looked like a rat on a leash," Mary said. "He would just slink along, doing this rat imitation, you know, tail between his legs, low to the ground, taking little, tiny steps. He looked just like a rat walking out into the light."

For the first few weeks, Mary concentrated on what scared Sota the most. When she opened the kitchen drawer and took out a spatula, she brought it close and showed it to him, laid it on the floor in front of him, stroked his legs and back with it until he stopped quivering. When friends came to the house, she urged them to talk to Sota in calm, soothing voices, and when they walked in the park, she let Sota sniff and greet the other dogs on leashes— most of whom were Randy's Stray Rescue dogs.

Mary also made it clear to Sota, through reward-oriented training, that she was the leader, so he understood and felt more comfortable with his place in the new pack.

Over the course of a year, Sota's nerves uncoiled, and he now entered the park with his ears forward and his tail high, tugging on the end of his leash.

"The hardest thing has been trying to get him to accept other people," Mary said as she looked down at Sota in her lap.

"He was never in a healthy situation, and then, when he was a stray, he reverted to being kind of wild. When that happens, their mistrust deepens, because they're constantly being teased, people throw rocks at them, chase them . . ."

She gave him rapid pats on the back as if to keep her thoughts from wandering to places she didn't want them to go. Then her forehead wrinkled.

"Look at him now, though," she said. Her voice shredded a little at the seams. "He's finding his way back."

Chapter Eight

The Evacuation

Heat danced in the air above the hoods of two cars parked in front of the warehouse as the early-summer sun rocketed down on the chrome details and sent shards of light in all directions. Because no one ever came to the warehouse, Randy circled and stared at the vehicles as if two time-delayed nuclear bombs were left there by accident.

He walked toward the warehouse, firing looks back at the two cars, and when he entered the coolness of the interior, he stopped and let his eyes adjust to the darkness.

"What you looking at?"

Randy sucked in air and backed up, as an old man—maybe not that old, but so grizzled and dirty it was hard to tell—stood up from the bed of pallets in the corner and crouched low, fists clenched, body as tight as a compressed coil. Despite the heat, he wore gloves, a watch cap, and a thick army coat over several layers of flannel shirts.

"Who are you?" Randy asked.

The old man spat on the ground. Randy stepped toward him. "Uh, my name's Randy. I feed—"

"I *know* who you are. You feed the coyotes." The skin on either side of the old man's eyes compressed into tight folds, and the edges of his mouth curved up. "And I bet you were born in *mausoleum,* heh, heh, heh."

Randy winced and fingered the bottom of his T-shirt as pigeons wrestled for balance in the rafters. Behind the man on the pallet bed, black flies spiraled over three sleeping bags balled up alongside piles of clothes, warped books, rusted pots and pans, old *Playboy* magazines, mismatched shoes, and newspapers that hadn't been there the day before. Two pigeons swooped down from the rafters. Randy ducked as they landed on the floor.

Randy turned and looked out the open door at the two cars. "Whose cars . . . ?"

"Party," the old man said. He leaned forward and pushed up off the bed with his gloved knuckles. "There's going to be a party in the mausoleums."

Randy sidled to the open side door and looked back and forth between the Quonset huts across the yard, and the old man, who clenched his hands behind him and paced back and forth beside the bed as if working out a sticky philosophical principle.

"Who's out there?" Randy asked. "Where are the dogs?"

The old man spat on the ground and kept pacing.

"Hey," Randy called across the space. "Hey, you . . ."

The old man stopped. He turned his head slowly, and when his eyes locked on Randy, he poked an index finger through the dusty air.

"My *name* is Lester."

He dropped his arm and spat again. "You got any smokes?"

Randy pulled a pack out of his front pants pocket, fished out one cigarette, and tossed it across the space toward the bed. The old man eyed it and smirked.

"Got a light?"

Randy pulled a lighter out of his pocket and tossed it too.

The old man grinned at the cigarette and lighter on the bed as if they had secrets he knew all about. Then he looked up at Randy.

"What's the matter, Coyote Man, afraid you'll catch something?"

"Have you seen the dogs?"

Lester shook his head.

"Whose cars are those?"

The old man picked up the cigarette, spat on the ground, and shrugged.

"They say the place *belongs* to them."

The sun arced over the Quonset huts as heat waves mixed with truck exhaust, river stench, and baked trash simmered in the yard above the weeds. Next to the Quonset huts stood a Dumpster the size of a semi trailer, and in front of the Dumpster, a man with wraparound sunglasses, black army boots, and pants that billowed from the lower half of his hips in apparent defiance of gravity, paced back and forth with a cell phone, at his ear.

"It's O-Tee, man," he said into the cell phone, as Randy waded through the weeds toward him. "I'm at the site, man, and there's shit *everywhere*. We're gonna need a, a, a whadda ya call those things, a bulldozer, man. My crew's doin' what they can, man, but like, you know, there's some funky, funky shit out here."

Randy stood by the Dumpster as the sound of scratching rakes filtered out from inside the Quonset huts.

"Just get one here, man, we've only got two days. . . . I don't know, man, maybe a hardware store, or try the fucking yellow pages, man."

O-Tee snapped the cell phone shut and looked up at Randy as if at the fifth disgruntled employee to stand in his office doorway that day.

"Yeah?"

Randy fingered the edge of his shirt. His own reflection stared back at him from O-Tee's sunglasses. "Hi, I, uh, I, uh, my name's Randy, and I um, uh, who are you?"

O-Tee's head snapped back. "You with the city or something? Because I got all the permits and insurance, yadda, yadda, yadda. The stuff is with my partner. You want his number?"

"No, no." Randy shook his head and shielded his eyes from the sun as he scanned the yard. "Did you see any dogs around here?"

O-Tee jerked his head back again. "Huh?"

"A pack of dogs lives here, and, uh, have you seen them?"

O-Tee's chin relaxed forward. "Oh, you must be the, what did he call you, the Wolf Man? I thought the crazy old fart was hallucinating, man. He kept blabbering about some guy who feeds wolves, or something . . ."

"Coyotes."

"Yeah, man." O-Tee bobbed his head up and down. "Coyotes, yeah. And he said stuff about how you were going to kill us all in our sleep or something if we fucked with the"—he waved his finger back and forth in front of him—"the whatevers."

"Coyotes."

O-Tee's head jerked up and down. "Yeah." He plunged his hand forward, toward Randy. "Name's O-Tee. I run a local production company. I'm hosting a DJ festival here on Saturday night."

"A what?"

"A DJ festival. Yeah, man. It's like a new style of rave. We're including hip-hop, so we're drawing the rappers as well as the raver crowd. But there's no gangsta rap. This will be fun stuff. We're bringing in Del the Funky Homosapien, Jay Biz of Hieroglyphics, Maseo of De La Soul. There's gonna be thousands of people here, man, *thousands*. Oh, man, that reminds me, I gotta call my partner."

He turned his back to Randy, flipped open the cell phone, and started pacing again. "Hey, it's O-Tee. I forgot, but we gotta get someone to pick up Jay Biz from the airport. . . ."

Randy tiptoed away from the giant Dumpster and into the middle Quonset hut. At the far end, silhouetted against the open back door, three kids with cigarettes dangling from their lips raked dried leaves into plastic garbage bags. They were younger than O-Tee, and as Randy walked toward them down the shadowy length of the Quonset hut, they stopped raking and introduced themselves as members of O-Tee's crew.

They were helping their boy O-Tee, they said, because they wanted to be a part of "the project." It was O-Tee's first big party, and they wanted to make sure it was a success.

O-Tee, the kid said, had rented the entire lot because it had "a lot of character." They expected two thousand people to pay $30 apiece to get into the all-night dance party. As the kid explained how generators would be brought in to power the lights and sound equipment, O-Tee, hand to ear, plowed through a herd of evacuated pigeons at the opposite end of the Quonset Hut.

"Come on, we gotta get this shit *cleaned up!*"

It had been a rough month for O-Tee, the crew said. In addition to dishing out thousands of dollars for a dance-hall permit, a building occupancy permit, and insurance, the twenty-six-year-old entrepreneur had handed out twenty thousand flyers, organized online promotional pages, and hired twelve security guards. He bought wristbands for the guests, linoleum for the breakdancers, and food for the VIPs, who included DJ I-Cue, DJ PMS, DJ Arson, and DJ Needles.

Randy's eyebrows shot up. "Where are you guys from, anyway?"

The kids shrugged and mumbled the names of several affluent westward enclaves.

"The suburbs?" Randy asked.

They offered half-smiles and looked at the ground and bounced their heads as if to cover all the possible implications of Randy's question.

For the next two days, Randy sat in the bus, parked across the street from the warehouse like a detective staking out a drug house. He chain-smoked and ate powdered doughnuts from a box in the mornings and chain-smoked and ate Sonic Burgers in the afternoons. He watched O-Tee's growing crew string lights, rope off parking space, and clear the yard of weeds and debris with a small orange bulldozer that they seemed to have trouble steering.

"It's like they think the city is a freak show," he said. "They think the dirt and the poverty and crazy, homeless people make good props for their party or something.

"This is the worst thing that could have happened. The dogs were in a routine . . . they *knew* I'd be there every morning, they *knew*, they could count on me to feed them, they *knew* there was at least one person who wouldn't hurt them, and now this."

The work on the Quonset huts seemed to stifle the ebb and flow of the whole street. First, the dogs disappeared; when the portable Johnny on the Spots came, Lester vanished, too. By the time the bulldozer had shoved a levee of dirt and trash up along the sidelines of the yard, even the old men with their shopping carts stopped their daily treks up the road. Maybe they'd tired of kids staring at them.

As if to still the fear in his stomach, Randy talked about his success stories above the bleating of cars in the yard, the shouts of kids in the Quonset huts, the back-and-forth drone of the bulldozer.

"Every dog can be rehabilitated," he said above the bump of flies bouncing off the front windshield and the dull whisper of distant traffic, police sirens, and helicopters. "There isn't one we've rescued who isn't learning to work things out.

"I mean, look at Sunshine. She was totally scared. She peed every time anyone came near her. But we just kept calming her, petting her, showing her new things. Then we taught her to walk on a leash . . ."

As Stray Rescue grew from what Randy described as "a bankrupt one-man freak show" into "a group of dedicated volunteers and a really cool Web page," more and more $25 and $50 checks landed in Randy's mailbox, along with donated bags of dog food, leashes, towels, blankets, and chew toys. New foster parents—people like Mary Zorich—signed up to volunteer daily.

The foster parents were the backbone of the organization. They dealt with the dogs fresh off the streets, still terrified and injured and crazy. Their ability to nurture troubled dogs and then hand them over to someone else permanently kept Randy from going insane. In addition, more and more prospective adoptive parents were filling out Randy's increasingly detailed forms.

At first, he gladly gave dogs to anyone who seemed kind, but he soon realized that even the most generous people sometimes had a hard time with what one ex-volunteer described as "psychotic mongrel monsters."

"It was like, these dogs would spend time in a foster home, get used to love and kindness, and become attached to a new family. Then they'd get sent to a whole new place. They didn't understand. They *liked* the place they were before, it was their new pack, so naturally they'd freak out, try to run back to the foster home, and pee on the carpets in complaint.

"So I make sure now that anyone who adopts a dog really understands what's in store. We charge fifty dollars for each adoption, which includes a spay or neuter and the dog's shots, and we counsel and cross-examine the adoptive parents until I'm pretty sure they want to shoot us."

But the tactic worked: more and more adoptions stuck.

Out in the warehouse yard, a car alarm went off when an empty city bus clattered by. Randy winced.

"Sunshine lives with a conductor of the St. Louis Symphony now," he said. "She's living like a queen."

O-Tee's crew flocked in and filled the giant Dumpster with tree branches, railroad ties, and shovelfuls of ancient black-and-green pigeon droppings. With the bulldozer, they flattened every bush and vine in the yard and threw metal poles and chunks of asphalt and shopping carts and wooden pallets on top of the piled-up brush and then flattened the yard again.

"This is horrible."

Trucks loaded with electronic equipment backed into the yard from the street, and as the kids directed them with hand signals toward the Quonset huts, the bulldozer razed a small stand of young trees.

"I hate them."

They set up hand-washing stations and unloaded boxes of flyers and planks of wood from their cars.

"They have no idea how bad this is for the dogs. Even if the pack comes back after all this commotion, all of the best hiding places are gone. I mean, it's like they're destroying an entire ecosystem."

They rolled the doors of the warehouse closed.

A group of three feral dogs (two males, one female) living in vacant buildings in St. Louis City was studied. They avoided close proximity with people and were active earlier and later

in the day than the people and loose pets in the area. They
found food while scavenging through human trash. The
group's activities were usually initiated by the female of the
group, though otherwise there was no clear linear hierarchy
and few ritualized displays of dominance or greeting.
Specific "roles" within the group were observable. Though
the female appeared to be pregnant during the study,
puppies were never noted.

When M. W. Fox, A. M. Beck, and E. Blackman wrote the above opening to their "Behavior and Ecology of a Small Group of Urban Dogs," in 1974, St. Louis had 600,000 human residents. By 2001, the population of the city had dropped to 350,000, and the number of stray and feral dogs, longtime residents believed, had more than doubled.

But no one knows for sure. Not in St. Louis, not nationally. No one keeps records of dogs who belong to no one.

While in the past several years, the federal government has addressed more and more animal-related issues—everything from standards for the humane slaughter of farm animals to the ban on steel-jaw leghold traps—it generally steers clear of pet overpopulation.

The problem has become increasingly apparent, though, and as America's cities clear out and nature reclaims lost ground, new licensing requirements, leash laws, and breed restrictions have sprung up locally like fertilized weeds.

In early 2000, the Los Angeles City Council passed a measure that upped the licensing fees for unaltered animals from $30 to $100. Furthermore, if Animal Control catches an unsterilized dog who is running loose, its owner could be fined up to $500. While the law is similar to other licensing laws across the country, critics—including the American Kennel Club—contend it will do little to help curb dog overpopulation.

Studies indicate, for example, that most unaltered pets are found in low-income neighborhoods where people have little or no access to veterinary services and can't usually afford any sort of licensing fee. In Los Angeles, fewer than 25 percent of dogs are licensed anyway. If sterilization is mandatory, private veterinarians may be less likely to offer discounted rates, and higher fees for unsterilized dogs may keep even more low-income owners from registering their animals. In addition, if an unaltered dog is caught running loose and the owner faces a $500 fine, the chances that the dog will be reclaimed at all are greatly diminished. The potential and probable consequence is that as low-income people—who tend to use large, unaltered, aggressive dogs for protection—leave their dogs in the city shelters, the demand for such dogs increases.

Breeding restrictions face equally heated opposition, especially from organizations such as the American Kennel Club and the National Animal Interest Alliance, a lobbying group composed of professional breeders, pharmaceutical research scientists, furriers, pet-store owners, and sport-hunting enthusiasts.

In 2001, following a trend across the country (and a fatal dog attack on a resident), lawmakers in Springfield, Massachusetts, debated a proposal to ban dog breeds considered aggressive or particularly dangerous. After intense lobbying by the American Kennel Club and the Massachusetts Federation of Dog Clubs, lawmakers dropped the idea. Breed bans were also defeated in the Maryland, Florida, and New Hampshire state legislatures in 2001. A California proposal to require the muzzling of certain breeds of dog in public places was also dumped in 2001.

Critics of breed bans argue that it is not the dogs who pose the threat, but irresponsible owners who don't spay or neuter and who train their dogs to be aggressive. Much like the National Rifle Association's argument that "Guns don't kill people; people kill people," the American Kennel Club campaign claimed "It's not the breed but the deed."

Usually at odds with the American Kennel Club, the national animal rights organization In Defense of Animals (IDA) also questions the effectiveness of breed bans. IDA's president and founder, the veterinarian Elliot Katz, argues: "Breed bans don't work, because it's difficult to decide what a 'breed' actually is. Most 'Pit Bulls,' for instance, are mixed breeds. They're not purebred Staffordshire Terriers. Besides, if a person wants an aggressive dog and there's a ban on Pit Bulls, then they'll go out and buy a Doberman or Mastiff instead."

Increasingly, Katz and others argue for measures that combine some enforcement with high levels of education. A measure signed into law in Colorado in 2001, for example, sets up the Companion Animal Overpopulation Authority, which will be funded with voluntary state income-tax contributions to study the issue. Other states, including New Jersey, Connecticut, Texas, Alabama, New York, Virginia, Louisiana, Arizona, and Maryland allow their residents to buy specialized license plates with a portion of the fee going to fund nonprofit shelters and spay-neuter clinics.

California is considered by far the most progressive state when it comes to animal-control legislation. In 2001, state lawmakers designated February 27 of every year "Spay Day USA" in hopes of bringing more attention to the growing problem of stray animals. It also proposed some of the following bills, which at the time of this writing were at various stages in the legislative process:

- A bill that would allow people who adopt dogs from shelters to deduct veterinary costs from their state income tax and allow veterinarians who perform free work on the animals to do the same

- A bill that would require pet shops to sterilize all animals before they are sold (shelters in California are already required to do this)
- A bill that would require that all dogs be microchipped for identification purposes and that the owner's name be placed on a state or national registry
- A bill that would fund signs warning motorists that abandoning animals on a highway is a crime
- A bill that would allow tax credits for sterilization costs

One component of the movement to address animal overpopulation is the idea that the law should view animals as *individuals* rather than as *property*. Katz of IDA, who is considered a leader in animal rights, believes that changing the term "animal owner" to "animal guardian" in legal documents will help change the relationship between people and animals.

"Right now they're recognized under law as 'property' that can be bought and sold as commodities," Katz says. "So people sell them and buy them and then get tired of them and throw them away. They buy them on the spur of the moment and make no long-term commitments to them, so that when they bite or bark or scratch something, they get dropped off at the shelter."

Katz and dozens of national and international animal organizations, including the Animal Legal Defense Fund, the ASPCA, the Jane Goodall Institute, and People for the Ethical Treatment of Animals (PETA), believe that dogs and cats should only be rescued or adopted, never bought or sold. If animals' legal status is elevated so that they care no longer "property," advocates hope, buying and selling will end.

So far, the state of Rhode Island and the cities of Boulder, Colorado, West Hollywood, and Berkeley, California, have enacted laws replacing the term "pet owner" with "pet guardian." The change will not have any actual effect on current laws, but it is hoped that it will at least tweak people's consciousness.

As the legal status of animals slowly changes, research into one consequence of animal overpopulation—namely, the existence of feral dogs—still depends pretty much on observations made thirty years ago. While more research is needed into stray dog populations, what was written in 1974 by Fox, Beck, and Blackman in "Behavior and Ecology of a Small Group of Urban Dogs" remains painfully pertinent:

Sometimes they were flushed out of abandoned buildings which showed signs of canid occupancy—feces, shed hair on old mattresses and carpeting, chewed food cans and cartons and toys, such as a chewed ball or stick. Putrefying and mummified carcasses of dogs were also found in some of these buildings.

The physical signs characteristic of many feral dogs were emaciation and skin lesions; some were in such poor condition that they were unable to run away when first located.

One was seen in the company of three free-roaming dogs and over a period of six weeks became weaker, more emaciated, and the skin lesions more extensive until it eventually succumbed.

Randy heard the music from his town house three miles away. It thumped and rumbled and boomed through the night like thunder from a distant storm. He turned up the TV. He closed the windows and clicked on the air-conditioning. He dug out his purple earmuffs from the back hall closet and wore them as he trudged up to bed.

"You're kidding, right?" Paul asked.

He held the pillow over his head; then he pulled the blankets up over the pillow. The rhythmic bass, *boom-ba-boom-ba-boom-ba-boom,* seeped in anyway, through the windows and the earmuffs and the pillow and the blankets, like noxious fumes.

"I can't take this."

Ten minutes later, he steered the bus around the potholes on Chouteau, and when he neared the warehouse, cars and campers and buses with license plates from six states hemmed him in. It took twenty minutes to travel the last three blocks to the warehouse yard. Cars filled every inch of parking along the way.

Kids streamed down the sides of Chouteau toward the Quonset huts, which throbbed in the distance like lit-up turbine engines. Kids in bell-bottoms, kids in tank tops, kids in bandannas, army jackets, baggy pants, platform sandals, knit watch caps, colored bead necklaces, and baseball hats. It was like trekking to Woodstock, only where bumper stickers plastered on Day-Glo school buses had once hailed Hendrix or the Stones or the legalization of grass, now bumper stickers covered $30,000 SUVs and endorsed ShadeFree, True Family Unit, and Voodoo Tribe.

The closer he got to the warehouse yard, the thicker the crowd became. It was like pushing the bus through a flock of baby vampires. In the yard, silhouettes twirled and swirled and swayed. Kids thronged toward the open doors of the Quonset huts, where flashing colored lights and sharp-edged laser beams shot through clouds of fog in time to the deep-gutted repeat of the primordial pound. *Boom-boom-boom-boom-boom.*

Randy stopped the bus at the yard entrance. The swarms swarmed in swarms all around it. *Boom. Boom. Boom. Boom. Boom.*

"I wonder how the pigeons are doing," he said.

The next morning, Randy traversed a sea of empty water bottles, party flyers, lost clothes, and jugs of Gatorade. In front of the Quonset huts, huge industrial fans, a Johnny on the Spot, and several wheelchairs lay on their sides; inside, mounds of cigarette butts and more water bottles and flyers littered the floor.

"Compton? Midnight?" Randy's voiced echoed as he walked through the three buildings. "Katlin?"

He walked along the back of the huts, where torn couches and chairs sat exposed in the sun.

"Bashful? Sunny?"

He tromped back to the main warehouse. It was embellished with new graffiti, and Lester's clothes and *Playboy* magazines had been trampled.

For the rest of the morning he walked the tracks, stopping at a train salvage yard where he thought he heard dogs barking. As he stood there, with a snare and a cigarette in one hand and a Baggie of braunschweiger in the other, a red-tailed hawk circled high above him. He called the dogs' names, and a rabbit scurried out from under a pile of steel beams and into a stand of low brush. Randy hooded his eyes and looked up at the hawk.

"It's like *Wild Kingdom* around here."

When the sun was high, he walked back to the warehouse, fired up the bus, and drove west to the oil towers, then east to Lafayette Square, then back to the railroad tracks that ran along the horizon under rippling ribbons of heat.

"This weather is as bad for them as the cold." He sounded as deflated as a week-old balloon. "They get dehydrated."

He stared out the cracked bus window and lit a cigarette, then leaned his head back and exhaled a loud stream of smoke.

"It still shocks me sometimes that other people don't feel the way I do about the dogs," he said. "When I first started doing this, I was surprised that other people didn't hear the dogs talking to them, you know? They tell you when they're hungry, when they're sad, when they're happy. I mean, they're just like us; they're living, breathing beings who search for happiness just like we do. They want comfort. They want a nice place to sleep, good food, and treats. They want to be loved and wanted.

"But, you know, I've realized that people choose not to hear them. People are selfish and don't want to see suffering. I mean, it's easier just to get rid of them, not to feed them, to kick them when they get in the way. Then it doesn't hurt to look at them, to hear them beg for help."

The next morning, Lester sat hunched and muttering over newspapers he smoothed and stacked in piles in front of him. As Randy walked in, the old man looked up.

"Messed up my stuff."

Randy nodded down at Lester but kept his eyes on the stacks of newspapers. "Have the dogs been back?"

Lester took the top newspaper off the stack nearest him and started a new pile.

"Have the dogs been back?" Randy asked. "Have you seen the dogs?"

The old man stood up, easing out the kinks in his back along the way, then dusted off his knees and turned and surveyed the warehouse like a farmer scanning a field of ripening corn. Then he squatted back down and sorted through the newspaper piles again.

"Messed up my stuff."

Randy left dog food at the warehouse every day for a week; every morning when he came back, the food was gone. But he didn't know whether the dogs, the pigeons, the rats, or Lester had eaten it.

"Crazy old man," Randy said. "I mean, how do I ask him if he ate dog food? What am I supposed to say, 'Did you by any chance see what happened to the *stuff* in the bowl?' 'Did you happen to accidentally put that *stuff* in the bowl near your mouth?' "

Growing frustration and fear ripened on Randy's face. "I mean, why does he have to be here, anyway? You'd think he'd rather live in a homeless shelter, where he'd at least get something to eat."

Randy sat on the tire rim, which had been shoved from the middle of the warehouse floor toward the open door. "If they're alive, they'll come back. This is their territory, their home base. They can travel for miles every day, so it would take them some time to get back. But if they're dead . . ."

His eyes widened as a thought broad-jumped into his head, and he looked out the door toward the Quonset huts.

"Maybe Lester *ate* them."

Two days later, Randy drove up to the warehouse and found Bashful, Midnight, Katlin, Taz, and Sunny sleeping in the scraped-down yard in the sun. When he leaped out of the bus and called to them, Katlin and Midnight dashed up and sneezed in excitement as their tails flashed back and forth like high-powered metronomes. Sunny stood up but kept her distance. Taz let out a perfunctory woof and waved his tail.

"Hey, gang, where you been?"

He reached out toward Katlin and Midnight, but they jumped back from his hand and wiggled and sneezed from a distance. Bashful stretched his long legs out in front of him in a gesture of welcome, as Sunny lay back down on the ground.

Taz woofed again, and Compton appeared in the open doorway of the warehouse with his ears forward and his tail high.

"Hey Compton, old buddy. Where you been?"

Compton stared across the yard at Randy and slowly relaxed his stance. With a movement not meant to be noticed, he shifted his tail left and then right.

"Who's hungry?"

Katlin and Midnight sneezed and pranced in place. Taz's ears pitched forward.

Across the yard, Lester's shadow fell from the doorway of the the middle Quonset hut, where he stood watching the pack follow Randy into the warehouse.

Chapter Nine

Bred in the U.S.A.

More than seventy miles stretched between St. Louis and the rural county near the foothills of the Ozarks. As the bus, followed by Dr. Ed's Blazer and a local television news crew's SUV, made its way to the edge of the city, a semi doing the speed limit roared past and sent the green bus careening to the side of the highway. Randy checked the rearview mirror to make sure the others were still behind them.

"You're doing forty miles per hour," Paul said from the passenger seat. "Where else on the road would they be?"

The bus followed the interstate beyond the sooty bungalows and "Bad Credit?" billboards out to the suburbs of grass and white brick. In the back of the bus, Caroline, a computer analyst and Stray Rescue volunteer, sat on a dog crate and swayed to keep her balance.

"How far is it?" she asked, as Randy swerved to avoid a spray of low-flying sparrows and the crates slid right.

Paul looked down at the map on his lap and shrugged. "It's about five or six inches on the map."

Twenty miles out, long, silvery shopping malls abutted churches that looked like federal buildings. Giant sports complexes, gated subdivisions, and car dealerships stretched along every horizon.

"It's creepy out here," Paul said.

Forty miles out, the highway carved through the flaky interiors of white limestone bluffs and ash, oak, and sumac ran riot on the slopes. Waffle houses, clapboard churches, goat farms, and lone trailers sat balanced on outcroppings of rock, and rugged gravel roads meandered into the hills. Billboards read "Abortion KILLS Babies!" and "Campground Ahead!" Here, in the middle of the state in the middle of the country, isolated roads, poor schools, rocky soil, and substandard health care barricaded the stagnant communities from economic development. The growth cottage industries were two: meth labs and puppy mills.

The Missouri puppy mills, mostly mom-and-pop setups, operate out of basements, sheds, and garages, and every month they pump out 12,000 puppies registered as purebreds with the AKC. Missouri puppy mills produce about a third of the nation's registered puppies every year. The state's central location in the country, its vast tracts of hilly, inaccessible backwoods terrain and its lax regulatory environment—regulators see the mills as a useful economic activity for commerce-starved rural areas—make Missouri the puppy-mill capital of the world.

As the caravan passed a billboard that read "Come See Elvis' First Car at the Elvis Presley Museum! Two Miles Ahead!" Randy checked the rearview mirror again.

"I can't believe we're doing this," he said.

Three days earlier, he'd gotten a call from a woman who said that her mother—who raised Beagles to sell at flea markets—had fled town for unexplained reasons and left behind "a whole mess" of dogs now locked up in a trailer. When Randy suggested she call the local authorities, the woman laughed and said that wouldn't work. When he told her to call the Humane Society of Missouri, she said she had, repeatedly, but they never showed up.

"Could be they couldn't find the place," she said. "We're kind of out of the way. But whatever, they haven't been here, and the dogs, they're dying in there, and me and my husband don't know what to do with 'em."

Randy called the Humane Society of Missouri himself and was promised for two days that it would try and get someone to the trailer. When the woman with the Beagles called back and told Randy that they still hadn't showed, he called Dr. Ed. Ed and his veterinary technician, Carrie, agreed to give up their Saturday and drive down to the trailer with him.

They met at Dr. Ed's clinic that morning, and a young reporter— Dr. Ed had suggested he should document the puppy mill issue, but he made Randy nervous because he kept saying "Look at *me,* not the camera"—asked Randy to explain why a group that rescued stray dogs off city streets was driving to the edge of the Ozarks to save a few Beagles out of a trailer.

The reporter pushed a microphone close to Randy's mouth as the camera lens whirred for focus. Randy fingered the bottom of his shirt.

"They, the puppy mills, breed them, um, the females I mean, like, uh, like twice a year. They just keep them in a cage their entire lives, um, to pump out as many, you know, puppies . . . huh?"

"Look at *me.*"

"Sorry. The camera is scary, but um, uh, but do you see where I'm going with this? They sell them, the puppies I mean, on the Internet or to pet stores. There's this one pet store we go to every weekend to get the puppies they throw away in the Dumpster, the ones I guess they can't sell, but, uh, that's another story. Sorry. Anyway, people see these cute little things in the pet stores, or wherever, and um, you know . . ."

The reporter jabbed his index and middle fingers in the shape of a V over his eyes.

"Sorry, sorry. Look at *you*. Right. Anyway, uh, they just buy them on impulse. I mean, impulse. Sorry, it's the camera. Can you, you know . . . can you . . . are you going to, you know, edit the stupid parts out?

"Uh, what was I saying? They buy them without knowing how much it's going to cost to get them vaccinated or spayed or neutered, and the puppies grow up and become a nuisance to the owners and, uh, you know, end up getting dumped at a shelter or in a park or on the side of highway."

The reporter stared at Randy and said nothing, as if still waiting for the point to be made.

Randy shrugged and kicked the side of one boot against the other, back and forth.

"And besides . . . who *else* is going to save them?"

The son-in-law of the woman who had abandoned the Beagles led the group—Randy, Paul, Caroline, the reporter, the photographer, Dr. Ed, and Carrie—up a hill toward the trailer, looking back several times to make sure the camera still had him in focus.

"Like I was sayin', we own this place, and people rent the space around the lake for their RVs."

The son-in-law looked at the cameraman and then pointed to the lake.

"So you can see why I don't want no dogs howlin' like they been doin' for the past couple days. Bad for business. Really bad. And there was dead dogs everywhere, under the trailer, near the lake . . ."

"Why'd she leave them?" Randy asked.

The son-in-law stopped, looked past Randy toward the cameraman, and planted his hands on his hips. Indignation blazed in his eyes. Then he shrugged.

"Dunno."

"How many are there?" Dr. Ed asked.

"Lots. This morning I finally kicked the door in 'cause I couldn't stand the howlin' no more, and a bunch ran out and into the woods." He took one hand off his hips and directed the camera lens toward the trees. "They was the ones loose inside. Then I let a bunch out that were tied to the walls."

"Tied to the walls?" Paul asked.

The son-in-law's eyes darted to Paul's stud earring. "Uh, yeah." Then he started back up the hill.

"Why were the dogs tied to the wall?" the reporter asked.

The son-in-law stopped and gazed into the camera again. "Oh, she bred 'em that way. Only way to keep 'em still, I guess. I don't know. She was kinda . . ." He twirled his index finger in tight circles at his temple.

As they got near the trailer, a thin Coonhound chained to a stake in the yard lifted its head off the ground. He let out a weak woof, then laid his head back down.

The group trudged toward the top of the hill, where several Beagles lay under the trailer and several more sat near the edge of the woods. Thinness pulled the skin taut over their ribs. Mange, dried feces, festering wounds, tumors, and pus from eye infections matted their dull, flat coats. They stared out from under the trailer. Blank. Noncommittal. Like institutionalized depressives.

As Randy bent to pet the Coonhound, the son-in-law stepped over the dog and opened the lid of a large wooden box, then scowled, backed away, and pointed inside.

"She bred kittens for the flea market in there."

Randy peered into the box with the cameraman and reporter behind him.

"She kept six to eight cats in there at a time," the son-in-law said. "When she left, she locked 'em all in the trailer with the dogs."

"Jesus," the reporter said, putting a hand over his mouth and backing away from the box. Four inches of hard-packed feces covered the bottom.

"That's nothin'," the son-in-law told the camera. He grinned and walked backwards toward the trailer door. "Wait till you see what's inside."

On November 12, 1997, WTNH-TV Channel 8, in New Haven, Connecticut, a special report opened with this statement: "Some puppy mills in the Midwest are supplying pet shops throughout the Northeast. That in itself may not seem bad, but what we found in Missouri will disgust you."

The reporter, using a hidden camera, traveled to several Missouri puppy mills, where he found the bodies of dead dogs rotting in small cages next to live dogs; wire cages stacked one on top of another so that when a dog on top defecated, the feces dribbled down through the cages below; and dogs so malnourished, filthy, and weak that they were "past the point of cleaning themselves."

Ninety percent of the 500,000 puppies bought in pet stores every year come from puppy mills such as this, according to the American Society for the Prevention of Cruelty to Animals, the Humane Society of the United States, and several other national animal-welfare groups. Licensed by the U.S. Department of Agriculture, these breeders are in the business—the very big business—of producing as many puppies as they can, as fast as they can, and as cheaply and easily as they can.

In 1996, a correspondent for the *New York Post* inspected numerous facilities owned by Amish and Mennonite breeders in Pennsylvania and found "a hellish world of filthy, crowded cages." Puppies with feces-matted hair were crammed into cages in dark sheds and basements; the animals were so despondent that they didn't acknowledge the reporter's presence or voice.

In 1995, the *Philadelphia Inquirer* reported that "the floors of many kennels are covered with urine and feces, and the kennels are sometimes contaminated with viruses. At times, waste is allowed to collect for days. The dogs' hair grows matted. The animals receive minimal contact." Further: "Feces had built up under the cages; cobwebs had grown in corners; some food was moldy; and several shelties had maggots beneath their coats. The odor was inescapable." The report went on: "Many of the dogs lived in total darkness, while others splashed around in mud tainted with their own excrement."

In 2001, *The Dog Owner's Guide,* a bimonthly newspaper, described a puppy mill this way: "The dogs are emaciated. It's evident that they spend a good part of their time hungry. There is no clean water, no dry, clean place to sit down. The dogs are filthy, their coats full of urine and feces. Because of the filth, there are flies; most of the dogs have missing pieces of ears, eaten away by the flies. Where there is water, it is mostly green."

Not surprisingly, only half of all puppies born in puppy mills survive to eight weeks of age, and half of the survivors who make it to pet stores become ill soon after being purchased. Puppy mill puppies not sold to pet stores are kept alive to breed more. Even in the pet shop, the puppies are isolated from regular human contact, fresh air and exercise, and other dogs, so by the time a pup gets into someone's home, it is likely to be plagued with physical and psychological disorders. Worms, upper respiratory infections, parvo, distemper. Careless breeding results in hereditary woes: epilepsy, aggressive behavior, autoimmune disorders, and hip dysplasia.

Puppies obliged to eliminate in their cages can be extremely difficult to housetrain. Dogs with problems like these often end up in local shelters or out on the street, and Randy and people like him mop up what they can of the mess.

The U.S. Department of Agriculture requires licensed dog-breeding operations to obey the regulations of the 1966 federal Animal Welfare Act.

But the USDA, whose goal is to support the economic welfare of the agricultural community, devotes few resources to the regulation of puppy mills. "Our inspectors are stretched pretty thin with 65 inspectors nationwide and almost 11,000 facilities to inspect each year," one USDA official wrote in response to a complaint. And according to the department's 1998 "Report to Congress," only 55 percent of the licensed facilities in the country complied with federal standards.

The federal standards themselves don't seem to make the inspectors' job any easier. Here is the Animal Welfare Act's outline of the minimum amount of floor space that is supposed to be dedicated to each dog: "Find the mathematical square of the sum of the length of the dog in inches plus six inches; then divide the product by 144. The calculation is: (length of dog in inches + 6) times (length of dog in inches + 6) = required floor space in square inches. Required floor space in inches/144 = required floor space in square feet."

As Peter Wood, the research director for People for the Ethical Treatment of Animals (PETA) stated in a letter of complaint to the USDA, "It is difficult to imagine a USDA inspector taking the time to actually confirm the adequacy of cage size given the ridiculous calculations set forth by the Act."

In Missouri, which has the highest percentage of licensed commercial dog breeders in the country, the Missouri Department of Agriculture (MDA) is responsible for overseeing compliance with state breeding laws enacted in 1992. The MDA, however, held not one administrative hearing concerning a Missouri facility, nor did it issue any fines or revoke any licenses between 1992 and the beginning of 2001.

According to a scathing report issued by the Missouri state auditor in February 2001, "This has occurred because program officials believe they should work with commercial breeders to improve operations instead of levying fines and revoking or suspending licenses. . . . Program officials stated that their role is to help facility owners correct problems and allow owners to use funds that would have resulted from fines to improve operations of the facility." The audit went on to state that the management philosophy of the MDA "favors commercial breeders, and effective procedures for inspecting facilities do not exist."

The report pointed out that there were "appearances of conflicts of interest of top management" at the MDA; for example, the program coordinator and an inspector—who were both responsible for the canine inspection program—were both former commercial breeders themselves; at the time of the audit, their breeding businesses were being run by their wives.

Laxity in proper regulation trickled down. The audit pointed out that *"federal* inspectors reported violations such as improper wire flooring, which could injure canines' feet; medications that had expired; canines that had not been properly identified; and enclosures that had not been cleaned. *State* reporters did not report any of these violations."*

In response to the audit, the MDA officials who ran the inspection program stated that federal inspections were "unreliable" and "nitpicky."

_____

*Emphasis mine.

The smell of urine and feces hit them first, slapped them in the face like a pair of angry hands. When the visitors climbed into the trailer and the stench of rotting food and flesh reached them, they covered their mouths in unison and gagged.

"Oh, my God," Caroline said as she doubled over and searched for air.

"Oh, man," the reporter said.

Randy turned in circles as if looking for a way out. "Sons of bitches," he said.

Dull light filtered in through ripped blinds and onto overturned furniture, dead mice, molding feces, rotting food, urine-spattered walls, bloodstained sheets, shredded cushions, balled-up clothes, and wall hooks with short metal choke chains attached.

"See?" the son-in-law said. "I told you they was chained to the wall."

Several starving cats skittered under a couch and stared out from beneath as if the human race and its cameraman—standing there in the doorway with sunlight and rescue streaming in behind them—were nothing more or less than the same stale air they'd been breathing for the past seven days.

"Look," Dr. Ed said. He pointed to the windows where the Beagles had torn at the blinds and gouged trenches at the sills trying to get out.

"Yeah, look at this place." The son-in-law held out his hands, palms up, as if pleading bankruptcy to the camera. "It'll cost me a fortune to clean it all up."

The photographer flicked on his camera light, the reporter shook himself from his stupor, and the son-in-law uprighted a chair.

"Uh . . ." The reporter stared down at his microphone and then moved it unsteadily toward Randy. "Is this the worst you've ever seen?"

Randy and Dr. Ed looked at each other across the room. They'd seen worse, but it all came from the same vat of spoilage. Randy raised his eyebrows, nodded at Dr. Ed, and inhaled for the first time since entering the trailer.

"Okay, let's get them out of here."

It took less than ten minutes to catch the cats and get them out into the yard, where the Beagles cowered low and trembled as if the sky and the clouds and the sun might at any minute swoop down and beat them over the heads.

"It seems like they've never been outside before," the reporter said as the cameraman knelt down and panned the yard and Randy scratched a Beagle between vague eyes.

"They probably haven't. Their only purpose in life is to produce puppies, and no one cares about their quality of life. They're not thought of as being *alive*; they're thought of as machines that make money. If you go to a puppy mill where they're kept in cages their entire lives, you find dogs who've never had physical contact with the ground or with people or with other dogs except when they're being mated. They don't even know how to play. Look at *them*," Randy said. "Do they look like they know how to play?"

A few of the Beagles crept on shaking, bent legs along the grass, noses instinctively down and forward. Others sat and stared.

When the trailer was cleared, everyone—except the son-in-law, who had stayed inside to fish a rat out of the toilet—grabbed a Beagle, and as they walked down the hill toward their cars, the other dogs slunk along on the ground close behind. Half of the Beagles, the Coonhound, and the cats went into crates in Dr. Ed's SUV; the other half went into the bus.

"What's next?" the reporter asked.

Randy's gaze swept the trailer park, the woods, and the surface of the lake. Places like this thrived because people used dogs, like cars, as measures of status, and whether they live in the suburbs and wanted pedigreed Labradors and Beagles, or in the cities, where purebred Rottweilers, Pit Bulls, and Chows fit the bill, they ended up, nine times out of ten, buying dogs born in places like this. Or worse.

What the new pet owners didn't realize when they forked over their $400 for the adorable little Boxer or German Shepherd in the window, was that their new puppy had had no healthy human contact, no normal interactions with other dogs, no proper veterinary care.

What was next?

"We get them the hell out of *this* place and back to St. Louis alive," Randy said.

They didn't all make it: one of the Beagles in Dr. Ed's Blazer had a heart attack on the way back. The unforgiving alliance of dehydration, malnutrition, and the shock of the trip wrung most of the life from the rest.

Inside, the clinic turned into a MASH unit. Randy and Paul sponged dried feces from the Beagles' coats as Caroline gave them water, and Carrie amassed thermometers, syringes, and bandages and placed them in the exam room, where Dr. Ed had not only shock and dehydration to tackle but also tumors, rotting teeth, heartworm, arthritis, eye infections, two pregnancies, periodontal disease, and skin disorders of every imaginable kind. They worked late into the night, bathing, cutting, suturing, and medicating.

As the last of the thirteen surviving Beagles, the Coonhound, and the cats fell asleep in their cages in the back of the clinic, Dr. Ed washed his hands at the sink, and Randy slumped against the wall, the need to keep them all alive was replaced by another need: to find homes for them all.

"What am I going to do?" Randy asked, sliding to the floor like the contents of a water balloon thrown against the wall.

Dr. Ed rubbed the back of his neck and shook his head. "I don't know."

The next morning, fueled by stress-studded exhaustion, Randy called the prosecutor from puppy-mill country and told him about the abandoned Beagles.

"What is it that you want from me, exactly?" the prosecutor asked.

"I want you to *prosecute* them."

The man at the other end of the phone didn't laugh outright, but his grin traveled the wire anyway. "*Prosecute* them?"

"Yes, I want you to prosecute them for animal abuse."

"*Animal* abuse?"

"Yeah."

"Do you honestly think I have the money to go around prosecuting folks for *animal* abuse?"

It had never occurred to Randy that the prosecutor didn't. Or that he wouldn't try. Or that he would find the conversation more than a little amusing. He experienced this same collision with reality when people told him that there were more important crusades than stray dogs or that dogs didn't feel their pain the way he did or that he couldn't save them all and that he shouldn't even try.

"I don't care," he said. "It's your job. This was a puppy mill just like hundreds of others in your county where the conditions are deplorable, and everybody turns a blind eye, and dogs suffer, and now I have to clean up your mess and find homes for thirteen Beagles, and unless you start prosecuting them, nothing is going to change—"

"Are you threatening me?"

"Huh?"

"*Are* you threatening me?"

"Uh . . ."

"I said, '*Are you threatening me?*'"

"No, sir."

"Good. I didn't think so. Now why don't you take your concerns about *animal* abuse somewhere else, because we've got more serious things to do 'round here than that."

Randy slammed the phone down, mumbled something about the prosecutor's lineage, and tromped to the kitchen for a carton of Ding Dongs, which he hoped would help him figure out what to do.

That night, before the five o'clock news, Paul, Randy, and his mother nestled in front of the TV and uncorked a bottle of Merlot. As the news music rose and the anchor announced that the top story of a puppy-mill rescue contained graphic scenes, Randy's mother whooped and filled each glass to its rim.

But what flashed on and off the screen seemed incomplete. Yes, there was the trailer. . . . There was the son-in-law's mouth. . . . There were a Beagle's pus-filled eyes. . . . There was a tumor. . . . There was—what *was* that? . . . There were Paul's shoes. . . . There was the box of cats. . . . There was Randy's huge, sweating, unshaven face, staring, mumbling something incoherently. By the end of the three-minute segment, Randy's hands covered his face, and he groaned.

The six o'clock news was as distressing as the five o'clock because in Randy's opinion it said nothing. It didn't clearly point out that puppy mills supplied animals bought on impulse at pet stores, which led to irresponsible ownership, which led to abuse and to loose dogs who weren't spayed or neutered, which led to millions of euthanized animals, millions more dying on the streets, hundreds of people bitten by aggressive strays, and Randy's current need to find homes for thirteen Beagles, a Coonhound, and a box of cats.

"But they never give three minutes to *anything* but presidential assassinations and big wars," his mother assured him.

"I thought you looked good," Paul said. "I don't think the camera really adds ten pounds at all."

By the ten o'clock segment, Randy was drunk. Near tears. The magnitude of the problem, its breadth and depth, its daily growth couldn't be captured on film or on paper, no matter how many column-inches or TV minutes it got. This wasn't the reporter's fault; the problem was just that bad.

But the phone rang the next day, and every day for the next two weeks. People wanted to adopt the Beagles. People wanted to donate money. People wanted to become foster parents. They wanted to meet Randy, to help him, to encourage him, because they hated the thought of living in the puppy-mill capital of the world and they thought he was a hero for pointing that out.

"I can't believe it," he said. "People *got* it."

For a few short weeks, things fell into place. The group had a foster home for every dog it found on the streets, a permanent home for every dog in a foster home, and enough money to pay its overdue bills at the kennels. One man called and said he'd donate the services of his public relations firm for whatever Stray Rescue needed. Another man called and said he'd like to donate a small building for a shelter.

And it helped. It helped for a few short weeks. Randy said maybe this was how revolutions started: one awful, three-minute sound bite at a time.

Chapter Ten

Cold Fires

Midsummer crept up on Randy. The allergy index, the smog warnings, the heat and humidity that made a person's skin feel covered in wet steel wool; they were all just suddenly there. But it was more than the season's sweltering discontent that ambushed Randy and grabbed him by the throat. Everything around him was changing.

For one thing, the news story about the puppy-mill rescue brought Randy and Stray Rescue out of the shadowy nonprofit sidelines and into the seared-white media glare. First there was a newspaper spread, then radio interviews, then other television news stories, then more radio. While the attention brought in publicity and donations, it was overwhelming too: if Randy had spent every hour of every day answering the phone, opening cards, and responding to e-mails, never eating or sleeping, and he still would not have gotten through all the work.

Besides, the publicity—and particularly the cards and e-mails and phone messages that declared him a "hero"—made Randy feel awkward in his own skin.

"They think I'm some kind of savior, but I'm not. I'm really not," he said. "I mean, if they knew this 'hero' had his groceries delivered because he can't even go to the store by himself without having a panic attack, they would know I'm not a saint. I mean, if they knew how paranoid I am about food . . . and flesh-eating diseases . . ."

Several weeks after the puppy mill rescue, the attention sent Randy into a fetal position on his couch, saying he couldn't take any more praise. He sat under a blanket—blinds drawn, air-conditioning turned to 45 degrees, fire lit—and watched the phone ring. He sat there the whole day. Once the sun went down, he said, he felt fine.

"Some hero. All this attention makes me feel like a fake, like I should go out and rescue a bunch of dogs, so I'm worthy of it somehow. I'm not a hero. I'm just doing what everyone should be doing."

The heaviest burden of the publicity, though, was the number of calls that came in from people pleading for help with stray dogs.

"They call because they saw this dog on the side of the highway and picked it up and then didn't know what to do with it," he said. "It's like, people will care up to a point, and then when they realize that the dog has fleas, they call me.

"I tell them I can't take in any more dogs right now, that I don't have any more adoptive or foster parents, and they get mad at me. They actually yell at me like *I'm* the one who dumped the dog."

Another major change from the way Randy wanted things to be was that O-Tee's first DJ festival had been so successful, he and his crew and his thousands of friends now invaded the Quonset huts every other weekend. They came in on Thursdays and swept out the garbage from the party before; then they chased Lester back into the warehouse and the dogs back out onto the streets. By Sunday morning, when the latest party was over and the last of the kids straggled back to their cars, the yard and the huts and the warehouse were sown with a new layer of cigarette butts, plastic water bottles, flyers, and wristbands, which wouldn't disintegrate for at least the next 10,000 years.

Then it started over again. Every time O-Tee's platoon landed, the pack escaped to wherever it was they went when they got scared. Randy always tried to find them, but among so many empty buildings, abandoned cars, and vacant fields, it was like searching for lost lottery tickets in a landfill.

"Every time they scatter, I think it's the last time I'll see them," Randy said one afternoon as he kicked through water bottles in the warehouse yard.

"When they're on the run, they have to deal with so many hazards, you know, cars and people and trying to find food, that it weakens their unity as a pack. They have to spend so much time just surviving that they can't concentrate on being a pack. But being a pack is the only thing that protects them."

He worried most about Katlin. She was the weakest female now and vulnerable to falling behind. "Being alone out there means you're a dead dog walking," he said.

But the pack always straggled back. The warehouse, the food, and Randy's attention were the only consistent things they knew, and by each Tuesday or Wednesday after the parties, he found them waiting in the coolest shadows of the yard.

"Hey, gang," he greeted them one morning as they assumed their spots of rank. "Where you been?"

Katlin bounced up first and met him with short sneezes and rapid tail wags of excitement. Midnight, ears forward but leery, circled close behind. Taz let out two warning barks but then joined Bashful and Sunny on the outer ring of Randy's presence as Compton stalked back and forth on the border. The stiff-legged leader guarded the distance between him and Randy as if it were a no-fly zone and only moved closer when scents of braunschweiger wafted from the Baggie.

"Look," Randy said as Compton moved on slow, deliberate legs toward him through the pack. "See how the rest of the pack lets him through? No matter how many days they've gone without food, they still let him eat first."

Randy tossed Compton the first glob of meat, then threw out pieces to the others. Until he rescued them all, he wanted them to maintain their pack structure, so he fed Compton first but let the others eat right after.

Except for Katlin, the rest of the pack looked at Compton before they ate, not with direct stares but with quick glances to see where his tail hung, where his ears moved, where his eyes chose to rest. Katlin threw no glances Compton's way but dove for the food like an ill-mannered only child.

"She's no longer deferring to him, and in some ways that's dangerous," Randy said. "She's changing her allegiance, which means that when I'm not around or they're out on the streets, she won't be as safe as the rest. Timing is important. I've got to save her soon."

With O-Tee's parties threatening the stability of their home base, Randy considered trapping the entire pack at once. But despite Stray Rescue's growing number of volunteers, there still weren't enough people trained to deal with the emotional demons that would possess these dogs when they first entered captivity, and Randy didn't have the time or the space to do it on his own.

"I don't even have time to be *here*," he said, and turned down the cell phone that screamed in his pocket.

As Randy watched the pack's cohesion deteriorate, another change affected his work with the dogs: Lester moved into the warehouse full-time.

"Tired of moving my stuff," he grumbled as he tossed a pair of boots up against the wall.

"But, you know I come here every morning to feed the dogs," Randy said. Panic squeezed his voice tight.

Lester turned and stared at Randy, and then he winked.

"I know everything about you, Coyote Man."

Locusts sang from invisible places, and a migrating flock of starlings cackled like applause in the warehouse yard. Soon, the nights would cool, the leaves would change, and the last of the massing birds would travel the river's flyway. But for now, summer clung like an outgrown suit.

With the weekend parties in full swing and with Lester living in the warehouse, the pack disappeared for longer and longer stretches. When they returned, they were thinner and scabbier, limping and weak, as if just released from boot camp or some hinterland prison.

"See how Katlin won't take her eyes from me?" Randy said as he stared back at her. Her eyes rounded like coins, and she blinked when she stared at him to indicate her low status. While the rest of the pack still watched Compton for their cues, Katlin ignored him and sat on her own.

"She's distanced herself from the others and is looking to me for help. Only she doesn't understand yet that she can totally trust me, so when I try to get near her, she still shies away.

"I've got to get through to her before the weather gets bad."

For the next week, Randy devoted all his attention to Katlin. He offered her extra braunschweiger from the tip of his finger. He spoke to her, to the exclusion of the others. When Compton signaled that it was time to leave, Randy pulled out more meat for Katlin, so she stayed with him alone, for just a few minutes while the others took off for the tracks.

One afternoon just before dusk, when frogs and locusts chanted in the yard, Randy walked into the warehouse and found Lester rocking back and forth on his bed as if in pain.

"Hey," Randy said when he walked in, "you okay?"

Lester sat up, stared at him with watery, uncomprehending eyes, then lay back down and rocked. Since the pack wasn't there, Randy poured dog food into the bowls, keeping an eye on Lester, and when he finished, he walked close to the bed and knelt down.

"Hey, Lester, are you . . . sick or something?"

Lester's head shook back and forth on the bed. "No more than you, Coyote Man."

Randy stood up and shrugged. "Have you seen the dogs today?"

Lester's head shook back and forth again. Then he turned his eyes up toward Randy and the edges of his mouth jerked up.

"They always come back at night."

Randy fingered the bottom of his shirt and shifted from one foot to the other. "They sleep in here with you at night?"

"Yep. I let them sleep by the fire. We talk."

"You talk?"

"Yeah, Coyote Man. They tell me all about hell."

Randy nodded and stepped backward toward the door. "I have to go."

"I know," Lester said, as he jutted his chin toward Randy and squinted his eyes.

Licking, grooming, tail wagging, hunting, playing, and posturing are as important to establishing bonds in a wolf pack as picnics, pow-wows, religious pilgrimages, high teas, soccer games, bedtime stories, and wedding ceremonies are to humans.

In a wolf pack, bonding starts when a pup is born. He cannot see, hear, or defecate on his own, and his brain waves are almost as flat as an adult's in deep sleep. His earliest attachment, to his mother's teat, is thus very influential, and the bond formed between mother and puppy will dominate the next several weeks of his life.

At about fifteen days old, the pup seems to have little fear of strangers, and he will approach other animals, including human beings, with curiosity.

By twenty-eight days, the wolf pup can see his litter mates, can hear other pack members growl, and understands that if he licks and paws at the sides of his mother's mouth, regurgitated food will come out. At this point, the mother is the caregiver and the pup is the dependent, and this constitutes the structure of his social life. Now when unfamiliar animals approach him, he is more afraid.

Soon, the mother walks away from him when he tries to nurse, then nips and growls when he pushes too hard, and he slips off the parent-child hierarchy of care-dependence and into the dominance structure of the pack as a whole. He learns that if he licks and paws at the sides of some adults' mouths, they will regurgitate food; others will not. He learns that if he shows his teeth, raises his hackles, and barks at one of his litter mates during play, the other pup rolls on its back, exposes its neck and belly, and grins submissively with its lips pulled back.

At the same time, the pup engages in more and more pack activities: running, howling, sleeping, eating, and grooming. As the bonds with his pack grow stronger, however, he becomes increasingly fearful of strangers, whom he learns to view as predators, prey, or territorial rivals.

In the wild, a small wolf pack is much like human family, which consists of a mating alpha couple and their offspring at various stages of maturity. Sometimes a pack includes several families of mating alpha pairs and their offspring, and sometimes the pack adopts an outsider as a subordinate member, or an outsider enters the pack and takes the place of a dead alpha. Because there is a constant repositioning of status in the pack as a pup grows into adulthood, he learns to calculate where he falls in the dominance-submission order of the group on any given day.

He learns the rituals, the habits, and the behaviors that weld the group together. Every morning when the pack members wake up, they greet each other with sniffs, play bows, licks, whimpers, and tail wags. Then, when the alpha male signals to the others that it's time to hunt, they coordinate their efforts, fall into line, communicate their strategy through eye contact, tail positions, and nose points, and carry out the plan. (Most wolves live with their "home" pack for at least three years before heading out on their own, and some researchers believe this is the amount of time it takes for a wolf to learn to hunt well enough to make it on his own.)

Similarly, all greetings between pack members seem to follow a routine. David Mech observed, for instance, that when the breeding male of a pack returns from hunting, the breeding female greets him in a "typical subordinate posture: with the tail down or between the legs, body crouched or on the ground, ears back, and nose pointed up, and licking the male's mouth. . . . The male stands there nonchalantly, sometimes raising his tail horizontally." Then, if the male has food, he drops whatever is in his mouth, and the female eats it herself or gives it to their offspring.

These rules or acts of bonding are almost as important to an individual wolf as eating, drinking, and breathing. By not understanding or adhering to them, the social animal faces eviction, solitude, starvation, or defensive attacks waged by members of other packs, which he will spend the rest of his life trying to join.

The normal course of a domesticated dog's life is different, because human beings slip in and replace the pack when the puppy is about eight weeks old. For a canid living in the wild, this is the time when the pup transitions from the care and dependence relationship with his mother to the submission and dominance structure of the pack. The dog, therefore, normally learns to incorporate humans in the dominant-submissive part of his social life.

But dogs born on the streets or abandoned by humans when very young face barriers to socialization with both human beings and other dogs. First, they are rarely born into a healthy, functioning pack where group roles and bonding rituals are clearly delineated, so things such as cooperative hunting and rearing of offspring are like customs from a foreign culture.

Secondly, if they do not bond with humans between four and twelve weeks of age, if they don't play, eat, or sleep with humans during this critical socialization stage, they, like most wild animals, will view humans with fear and suspicion for the rest of their lives.

Soon, even the changes changed. By the beginning of September, when the light over the yard softened to dappled gold and white, and birds massed, and the weeds stiffened and dried and rustled in the wind like crinoline, O-Tee's parties ended and left in their plastic-strewn, psychedelic wake a bruised and battered disruption of the way Randy wanted things to be.

He blamed the parties for the detailed list of everything that was wrong. If it weren't for the parties, he reasoned, things would be as they had been: Lester in the Quonset huts, the dogs in the warehouse, and quiet in his head as he communed with the pack every morning. With the conviction of the newly born-again, he decided that if it not for the parties, Katlin would already have been rescued, and if Katlin had been rescued, he'd sleep better, eat better, and be a better person. He'd focus on Stray Rescue's sudden popularity, return every phone call, and send his mom flowers on her birthday. He would exercise, pay the accountant, answer his e-mails, see the dentist, paint the town house, and design a training manual for his neglected volunteers. He'd clean out the bus.

As summer closed, the cold fires in the warehouse escaped Randy's notice until he pulled up one morning and found a man peering into the open doors.

"Who's *that?*"

The man, dressed in a loose tie and tweed jacket too short in the sleeves, smiled as Randy jumped out of the bus.

"Hi." The man rearranged the plastic bags of groceries in his arms and extended a free hand. "I'm looking for an old man who stays around here."

"You mean Lester?"

The man's eyes widened and he smiled again. "So, you know Lester?"

Randy's forehead wrinkled with suspicion. "Sort of."

"I'm his caseworker. I haven't seen him in a while, and I was a little worried. Have you seen him lately?"

Randy looked over the yard in brisk circles, as if he just realized something was missing.

"No."

"Do you know when he was here last?"

"Uh, no, not really, maybe a few weeks ago. I really don't re-member. I, uh, I don't come here for him. I mean, I don't help him, I mean, I feed a pack of dogs who live here, and he, Lester, he kind of scares me, you know, he seems, um, seems confused or some-thing, so I . . ." Randy shrugged.

"It's okay," the caseworker said. "Lester *is* confused, but don't be afraid of him. He's totally harmless, believe me. He's much more scared of you, I'm sure, than you are of him. He's been through a lot. He's a Vietnam vet, for one. . . ."

"He looks older," Randy said.

"Well, like I said, he's been through a lot. I've been trying to convince him to move into the facility that I work for, because he can get work there, and he'd have hot meals and a warm bed, but he won't do it."

"Why not?"

The man smiled the sad, burdened smile of someone who understood the problems of others much better than they did themselves. And wished he didn't.

"Fear."

An arrowhead of geese followed the horizon. Spiderwebs trembled in a warm, sharp wind.

"So sometimes I bring stuff out to him," the man said. "Food, clothes, cigarettes. I want him to trust me, to know that he doesn't have to be afraid of me, and that can take a long time."

A shopping cart rattled up the street, and the locusts went wild in the yard.

Every morning for the next week, Randy checked the fire and Lester's bed before he called for the dogs, but the fire was the same pile of ashes it was the day before. The pack didn't answer his calls.

One afternoon, he walked into the warehouse and found another man—this one in two moth-eaten coats and fingerless gloves—yanking Lester's sleeping bags from the bed.

"Hey," Randy yelled across the warehouse, "that's not your stuff!"

The man crouched low, his arms went wide, and he froze, as if considering whether to steal second base.

"Get out of here. That's Lester's stuff."

In one fluid movement, the man swooped down, swiped one of Lester's butter knives off the ground, and dashed out the open doorway.

As Randy watched the man disappear down Chouteau, he sighed. "It's like Grand Central Station around here these days."

The next day, Randy found the pack in front of the Quonset huts, and as if they'd never been away, Katlin ran up to him and sneezed and wagged her tail, Sunny, Midnight, and Bashful hovered behind, Taz woofed a halfhearted alert, and Compton paced off on his own.

But this time when Randy reached out toward Katlin, she didn't jump back. Instead, she lowered her head, raised her right paw, and then rolled onto her back with her belly exposed and her face turned sideways to avoid eye contact.

Randy smiled and bent down over her.

"This is it, isn't it, girl?"

Katlin's dark eyes stared off, away from Randy, away from the rest of the pack, away from things she didn't understand. Her front legs curled over her chest and shook, but even when Randy's hand came close, she didn't pull away.

Randy looked down at her to cement his higher status but blinked to let her know the look wasn't a threat. He let his hand slide down her chest, then back up, then back down, over and over and over again until her front legs rocked with the motion of his hand and her lids drooped down as she relaxed.

"Don't be afraid now," he said as he brought the snare toward her head. "This isn't going to hurt at all."

Her eyes opened and her legs stiffened, but before she could roll and stand up, Randy slid the loop around her neck.

She pulled back and shook her head, but the snare tightened around her thick fur and pulled it forward around her face like the mane of a lion.

"It's okay, Katlin, it's okay."

Randy talked low and slow as he reeled in the snare. Katlin's legs stiffened and her nails dug into the dirt, but as Randy rubbed the base of her ear, then her forehead, then her neck, then her other ear, she loosened and then slumped to the ground.

It took Randy twenty minutes to get her to the bus and another twenty minutes to calm her once she was inside. "Everything's going to be fine," he said as he stroked the back of her neck.

When he pulled out of the warehouse yard, with Katlin perched on the blankets as if she'd ridden in buses all her life, Compton was sitting in the doorway of the warehouse, watching them leave.

"I wonder what he's thinking," Randy said.

As he wound down Chouteau toward Lafayette Square with Italian arias in the tape deck to soothe Katlin's nerves, Randy slowed at every side street and looked down each one for Lester.

Chapter Eleven

In the Deep End

"I can't stand this."

Randy knelt in front of the portable wire cage and watched defeat, in the form of a fifty-pound Rottweiler who should have weighed eighty, moving toward him by pushing his head along the floor with the force of his raised hind end.

"Don't, Louis. Don't try to move."

Randy stood up and walked away across the cement floor. Louis's high-pitched screams, *ar-ar-ar-ar-ar,* followed him in the chilly, open space.

The building—it had been a two-room machine shop and then one of the last derelicts in Lafayette Square—had been donated to the group several weeks before. Although it had no heat and no plumbing, and there were no windows in the cinder-block walls, Randy had set up two six-foot-high portable pens inside for emergencies like this.

Ar-ar-ar-ar-ar.

One of Dr. Ed's clients had found Louis crumpled in her yard two weeks before with his ears sliced, his throat cut, and his legs almost crippled from four poorly healed fractures. He'd either been dumped in the yard or escaped from someplace and made it just that far, and while he could walk when Dr. Ed first saw him, pain shot through every step.

He had offered no resistance on the way to the clinic. But when confronted by the white-smocked vet under bright fluorescent lights, he lunged and attacked as if jolted from a deep, troubled sleep.

Once muzzled, bandaged, stitched, and sedated, Louis crumpled back in on himself. A family offered to foster him during the recovery, but as he crawled his way back out of sedation over the next several days, he grew aggressive and attacked them as well.

"I brought him here to the building," Randy said. His words echoed in the empty space like an incriminating rebuttal. "He was on painkillers, but all he did was lie there and stare at the wall. I'd sit next to him and talk and talk, and after a while, he'd start looking up at me and wagging his little stumpy tail."

Randy lit a cigarette and stared across the room toward Louis, who edged one of his front legs out from under his chest. *Ar-ar-ar-ar-ar.*

"It was obvious he was trained as an attack dog, and then he was tortured and dumped on the streets, maybe he ran away, who knows, but he was afraid and in a lot of pain. I knew it was just a matter of being patient. I've never had a dog that didn't respond to heavy-duty kindness, that I haven't been able to get through to eventually, so I sat with him and fed him groovy food and told him how cool things would be once he learned how to be happy.

"And honest to God, he turned into a really sweet dog. One night, I sat with him, and he just lay there with his head on my lap whimpering like he'd never experienced being petted before. It was like he was crying in my lap with joy."

Randy pulled on his cigarette. Louis moved his extended front leg along the floor toward him.

Aaaaarrrr.

"But whenever I brought anyone else in here, he went crazy. He tried to attack everyone. He seemed to be getting physically better, and that's the first thing you have to deal with anyway. But this afternoon when I came in, he was all bent over and howling in pain. Now, even though he wants me to be in there with him, he tries biting, because the pain is driving him mad."

Louis pushed the side of his head against the floor behind his extended leg but kept his back legs pushed upright to take weight off his back, as if he were trying to eavesdrop on a conversation beneath the floor. As he lay there with his ear against the cement, his look crawled the distance toward Randy that his body couldn't, but every movement, even blinking, brought on more howls.

Ar-ar-ar-ar-ar.

Randy flicked his cigarette against the wall. "Man, I wish Dr. Ed would get here soon."

Pain was the worst kind of enemy. He couldn't see it, couldn't smell it, couldn't root it out and chase it away, and its well-sited shots could be deadly. As Dr. Ed stared down at the Rottweiler, who couldn't breathe without pain, the first trickle of sweat made its way down his face.

"What's *wrong* with him?" Randy asked across Louis's arched back.

Dr. Ed looked over Louis's body, but all he could see was the manifestation of pain. Despite his training—*Pain was the sensation resulting from nerve impulses moving through ascending neural pathways until they reached the cerebral cortex. . . . Neuronal input caused by noxious stimuli . . . Pain was all chemicals and electrical currents and impulses*—it was hard to see beyond it to how much pain *hurt*.

"I don't know."

It was late afternoon, and this was Dr. Ed's last task of the day. His wife, Mary, and their three daughters expected him home for dinner, but he had to get a sedative into the Rottweiler before he could move him to the clinic and better survey the damage.

As he opened the cage door, Louis bared his teeth and growled, then pushed his head along the floor toward the vet, challenging him despite the pain.

"He's big enough to do a lot of damage," Dr. Ed said as drops of sweat pooled on his forehead. "I just hope I can get a muzzle on him."

Louis growled but rolled lower onto his shoulder, *ar-ar-ar-ar-ar,* then bared his teeth again.

"Take it easy, boy, settle down."

Dr. Ed threaded a leash so that a looped snare hung from the bottom. Standing with his back to the open door, he leaned forward from his waist and dangled the noose over Louis's head. Randy's fingers wrapped around the thin wire bars from the other side of the cage.

Dr. Ed lowered the loop. When it touched Louis's nose, the dog's head came up and he snapped at the air. Dr. Ed jumped back. *Ar-ar-ar-ar-ar.*

The loop went down again, and again Louis snapped at it. *Ar-ar-ar.*

Dr. Ed stepped closer and tried again. *Ar-ar-ar.* Then again. *Ar-ar-ar.* Then again. But despite the agony that tore through him, each time Louis saw the loop come close, he tried to scare it away. *Ar-ar-ar-ar-ar.*

"*Stop.*" Randy flung himself away from the cage. "I can't take it anymore."

Sweat scrolled down Dr. Ed's face and disappeared under his collar. He shook his head and stepped backward out of the cage.

"The only way I can get the muzzle on is from behind, but with his back up against the wall like that . . ." He ran his palm along the back of his neck. "Randy, can you coax him out somehow?"

Randy eased into the cage, knelt in front of Louis, and held his hand out toward the Rottweiler's face.

"Come on, buddy, come on. Come with me, come on, you can do it."

Louis's nose twitched as his dark eyes stared up at Randy and blinked.

"Come on, Louis. Everything will be all right. I promise."

With his hand still extended toward Louis, Randy backed out of the cage on his knees.

"Come on, boy, come on."

Louis pushed his shoulders and head along the floor, *ar-ar-ar-ar-ar,* seeking Randy's hand. When he was clear of the door, Dr. Ed lowered the loop from behind him, maneuvered it around his nose, and yanked up. As the cinch tightened, Louis pulled away, but Randy grabbed the dog's head and cradled it as Dr. Ed plunged a needle into his shoulder.

Louis whimpered through the loop around his nose. Randy stroked his forehead. "Everything's going to be okay, Louis, I promise. Don't be afraid, everything will be fine."

While they waited for the sedative to wind its way through Louis's body, Randy held his head and scratched his ears. Dr. Ed knelt to watch his labored breathing.

"What's wrong with him, Dr. Ed?"

He didn't know. Diseases and injuries, causes and effects, they popped like flashbulbs in his head. But nothing went together, nothing gelled, nothing fit, and with the sweat still trickling down the side of his face, he shook his head and watched Louis breathe.

"He was getting better," Randy said. "He wasn't trying to bite me anymore. It's just the pain that makes him this way."

Dr. Ed leaned toward Louis and checked the dog's reflexes; the Rottweiler flinched and growled.

Behaviorally, this was an unpredictable dog with a history of biting and attacking, and while Randy had pushed Dr. Ed to perform miracles in the past, the miracles hadn't come cheap. In this case, the emotional, physical, and monetary indicators all predicted a downward spiral, but the problem, whatever it was, might give Dr. Ed the out he needed. . . .

Randy leaned down over Louis. "Everything's going to be okay, buddy, I promise. Don't worry, I *promise.*"

It was the climax of the rush-hour exodus from the city, but Randy wove the bus through the headlights and horns as if what stood between the donated building and Dr. Ed's clinic was a long, empty stretch of an old country road. Even though he'd forgotten his Xanax, he sailed past ambulances, ran red lights, passed stopped school buses, and tailgated. At one point, when he lost sight of Dr. Ed's Blazer with Louis asleep in the back, Randy ran the bus up onto the curb and blamed the scattering pedestrians for cutting off his lane change.

"You know," he said as he lit a cigarette and glanced in the rearview mirror at the bleating car behind him, "Dr. Ed thinks Louis is too mean to be adopted out, but he's wrong. He's wrong. He's really, really wrong,"

Randy leaned forward in his seat and his eyes bounced from the side mirror to the rearview mirror to the other side mirror.

"I mean, Louis is no different than, than, than, Matt, for instance, and no one thought Matt would *ever* find a home. I mean,

Matt was this Chow mix someone found on the highway who was really, really aggressive, and at the time, I couldn't find a foster home for him, because he tried to attack anyone who, who came near him, so I stashed him in my backyard, I can't remember whose, doesn't matter, maybe it was Ellie's, anyway, I would, would just go up to the fence every day to feed him and he'd pace back and forth like, like a lion in the zoo, you know how they pace like, like they're really pissed off at being locked up, that's how he was, and I'd, I'd just feed him through the fence every day until he started wagging his tail when he saw me instead of trying to kill me through the fence, and then one day I just went into the yard, and, and, and . . ."

As he threw his cigarette out the window, the bus swerved into oncoming traffic. He jerked it back, but the momentum sent it careening across his own lane and into the path of a screaming minivan, which veered into the curb.

". . . and I, you know, I just sat at one end of the yard and waited for him to come up to me, and he did eventually, I mean, it took a couple of days, but he became this great dog, and nobody had any faith in him but me."

He lit another cigarette.

"And then there was Sampson, who I found dying in a park—no, no, someone else found him in the park and brought him to the shop—no, to my house—but he was a huge German Shepherd, and he had big, huge chains wrapped around his body, there was even a padlock on it that we had to cut off, and his ears were bleeding from fly bites, and he was emaciated and so weak he could barely lift his head up, you know, he had that I-give-up look, I think he had heartworm, they all have heartworm, and, and, as he got better and got his will to live back, he started attacking people, not me, but other people, but when he was with me, he just, he just, he was so sweet and devoted. . . ."

Randy sped around a corner and the bus tilted on its axis. When the clinic came into view, he tossed his cigarette out the window and lit another one.

"Dr. Ed also thinks Louis is too sick. I saw it in his eyes. I know that look. But you know, I saw that look in his eyes when we brought Carly to him, who was this Rottweiler, just like Louis, who was like, like, like thirty pounds, and she was skin and bones, I mean, I never saw a dog as thin as she was, and she had a broken back and couldn't move, and, and her rectum was bleeding, and when Dr. Ed did X rays on her, he found—this is how hungry she was—he found puppy bones inside her stomach, she must have given birth to dead puppies and then ate them because she was starving to death, and I know he thought she was too malnourished and broken up, he wanted to put her down, and . . ."

He gulped for air. ". . . Dr. Ed told me how much the drugs for her would cost, and at the time, it was more than Stray Rescue's entire budget. But it didn't matter. She had suffered for months, and if there was any hope, it was worth it. And then somebody donated a big chunk of money, and, well, it always seems to work out in the end, you know, and now she's in a home and, I mean, she can walk and play and do almost everything any normal dog could do, but what's normal anyway? I mean, they're all pretty screwed up, I mean, I mean . . . Louis will be okay. I know he will. Louis will be okay."

He ran the bus into the parking lot of the clinic and parked next to Dr. Ed's empty Blazer. He shoved the gearshift into neutral and sat back in his seat and stared at the side entrance of the clinic. He stared hard. He checked his rearview mirror. He brought his cigarette up to his mouth. He checked the rearview mirror again.

"I don't think I can go in there," he said.

———

In 1998, animal-control wardens in Washington, D.C., found 515 stray Pit Bulls on the streets, and of that number, 426 had to be euthanized immediately because they were so aggressive.

In New York City in 1999, police shot a pack of Pit Bulls who attacked three boys in the Bronx. That same year, a pack of dogs surrounded and mauled a twelve-year-old girl in Los Angeles on her way home from school. One year earlier, in Pittsburgh, a toddler had been bitten by six dogs in the Beaver County public housing project; in Indianapolis, joggers carried broomsticks and baseball bats to fend off dogs in the parks.

Between 2000 and 2001, the following headlines appeared in various newspapers across the country:

"Pit Bulls Attack, Wound Three in San Jose Apartment Complex."

"San Francisco Police Fire 30 Bullets to Kill Pit Bull."

"Child Mauled to Death by Dogs."

"Census Worker Dead: Pack of Dogs Found Feeding on 71-Year-Old Woman's Body."

"Police Kill Dog After it Mauls Southern California Woman."

"Pit Bull Attack Ends With Man Choking and Then Drowning Animal."

"Three Students Hospitalized After Pit Bulls Board Bus."

Rarely are any attacks against humans launched by feral dogs, which are as afraid of humans as coyotes, wolves, or foxes. This means that most dog bites and attacks are made by people's stray pets. In one study conducted by Dr. Alan Beck, with the Center for the Human-Animal Bond at Purdue University's School of Veterinary Medicine, 65 percent of aggressive behavior exhibited by dogs on the street came from owned pets, while only 12 percent came from ownerless dogs; these generally fled when humans approached.

Between 1986 and 1994, the number of people who reported

being bitten by dogs increased by 37 percent, according to the Centers for Disease Control, and now almost 5 million people are bitten every year, with some nine hundred people ending up in emergency rooms every day. Health officials generally estimate that twice as many people who are bitten don't report the bite, and one study conducted by Alan Beck and Barbara Jones indicates that the number may be much larger than that.

The study points out, for instance, that on air force bases—where dogs are more tightly controlled than elsewhere, health care is free, and health reporting is more accurate—almost three times as many dog bites are reported as in the population at large. The researchers then interviewed thousands of school-aged children and found that (excluding bites initiated by play) a dog had bitten almost half of the students at some time in their lives and that only about 10 percent of those bites came from stray dogs.

The researchers were puzzled, though. Both among children and on air force bases, about a tenth of reported bites were inflicted by strays. But the reported bite rate from stray dogs in the general civilian population was almost double that, 20 percent. Why?

"The overreporting of bites from strays relative to owned dogs has probably been influenced by the belief that strays are less likely to have been vaccinated against rabies," the researchers noted. "Stray dogs may also have been seen as a continuing danger in the environment compared with owned dogs, which can be identified and restrained after a bite."

In another study, Beck points out that "most free-ranging dogs are actually straying pets. . . . In our field behavior studies, the truly stray animals were extremely shy of people, and we have never observed them acting aggressively towards people. . . . True strays have few defenders; thus, blaming strays for the bite problem shifts responsibility to no one."

The responsibility for human-killing dogs, however—an estimated twenty fatalities per year—can statistically be placed in the laps of their owners.

In 2000, five researchers conducted a study to find out what breeds of dogs killed people. According to the findings, 300 people died as a result of dog bites in the United States between 1979–1998—a number, which didn't include 90 deaths in which the breed of the dog or dogs who attacked was not known—and 67 percent of the deaths came from Rottweiler and Pit Bull–type dogs, with the Pit Bulls responsible for most. The team pointed out, however, that the report was not able to calculate owner-related issues. "For example, less responsible dog owners or owners who want to foster aggression in their dogs may be drawn differentially to certain breeds."

Also in 2000, the *Journal of the American Veterinary Medical Association* reported that for the first time, Rottweilers surpassed Pit Bulls as the deadliest dog breed in the country, accounting for thirty-three fatal attacks on people between 1991 and 1998. According to many animal-control experts, however, this may be the unintended consequence of bans in many areas on breeding Pit Bulls, because people simply find a replacement breed.

After the mauling death of Diane Whipple in San Francisco in early 2001 by two of her neighbor's mastiff/Presa Canario mixes, intense media attention was focused on the increasing popularity of owning large, aggressive dogs. While some reports initially focused on the aggressiveness of certain breeds, most eventually focused instead on genetics as manipulated by human training. The two dogs who attacked Diane Whipple, for instance, were reportedly being raised to produce guard dogs for methamphetamine labs in Mexico.

The trend toward buying bigger, more aggressive dogs for protection accounts for some of the increase in attacks—surveys indicate that 40 percent of all dogs are bought for protection these days—but numerous other factors must be added to the equation: 70 to 90 percent of instances of aggression involve male dogs who have not been neutered; pet store—or puppy mill—dogs display a high degree of antisocial aggression; the practice of training dogs for fighting or using them for bait and then abandoning them produces more aggressive strays; and chaining a dog has been shown to provoke aggression: 28 percent of all fatal dog attacks involve dogs chained in their yards.

A study conducted in St. Louis by the veterinarian Philip Wagenknecht indicates that intact (unneutered) male strays launched 90 percent of all reported dog attacks involving biting in the city during a ten-year period. In the year 2000 alone, 1,397 intact male dogs were apprehended by St. Louis City animal control and another 2,174 were caught by St. Louis County animal control.

Dr. Wagenknecht also interviewed 202 grade school students who lived in areas with large numbers of stray dogs and found that two-thirds of them had "experienced being approached, chased, or bitten by dogs and/or taken precautions while walking like carrying a stick, crossing to the other side of the street or have a family member walk with them to and from school."

Dr. Ed stared up at Louis's X ray as if searching a detailed wall map for a place he wasn't sure existed. There was Louis's backbone, a curved road that carried all of Louis's neurological commerce. There were the vertebrae, lined up like speed bumps. There was the neck junction. There was the skull. The problem hid somewhere in one of them or in several of them or in the spaces or lack of spaces in between.

"His stomach appears bloated." Dr. Ed traced his finger along a halo of soft tissue in the abdomen. "His hips look okay, but he's definitely got some instability in the back. It could be inflammatory meningitis, which is extremely painful, or look at this"—he tapped the image of the sixth and seventh cervical vertebrae—"see how the two discs are slightly compressed?"

Randy nodded. "What does that mean?"

Dr. Ed turned away from the wall and bent over the examination table, where *Diagnostic Radiology of the Dog and Cat* and *Radiographic Interpretation for the Small Animal Clinician* lay open. Above him, fluorescent lights hummed as he moved from book to book, fingered passages, nodded, read out loud ("a subluxation of the vertebrae involving the intervertebral spaces"), looked back up at the X ray, shook his head, then dove back down into the pages.

"It could be Wobbler's disease." He shook his head and flipped a page. "It could be lumbo-sacral stenosis, or a neurological deficit that I can't see. I don't know. I just don't know."

Randy still stared up at the X ray. "Can you fix it?"

Dr. Ed turned back to Louis's illuminated spine. "I could give him a blast of steroids, and see what happens in the morning; it would give him some relief from the pain, but it won't totally solve the problem. I think whatever it is it will require major surgery and a long recovery time, with no guarantees. Then he'd have to go through physical therapy every day, which would be very painful, and because he's so aggressive, especially when he's hurting, I'm not sure anyone could handle him."

"I could."

Dr. Ed's head bowed as he turned away from the wall and walked, with his arms crossed across his chest, in circles around the room. As a vet, he balanced on a jury-rigged line, life on one side, death on the other. Both tugged at his shirtsleeves for attention; sometimes, like tonight, death demanded to be heard. When that happened, no matter how much pain or expense or futility stood before the inevitable, he never told a client that there weren't any options.

He had to spell out the options first, though.

"Maybe you could handle him during physical therapy, Randy, but what then? He's an extremely aggressive dog. Even if surgery and rehabilitation are successful, who are you going to adopt him out to?"

Hope made a last stand on Randy's face. "I'll adopt him to someone who doesn't mind getting bit."

Dr. Ed arched his eyebrows. "If he attacks someone or kills a child, who holds the blame, Randy? Who holds the blame?"

"Are you saying I should put him to *sleep*?" Randy asked as he unwrapped the choice in his mind. "Are you suggesting that I kill Louis, because some *asshole* taught him to be mean and then tortured and abandoned him? Is that what you're saying? Because if it is, the answer is no. I have never had a dog put to sleep. Never. And I'm not going to now. No. We don't do this to a child if he's bad. No. I can't do it."

Dr. Ed leaned back against the examination table and let the differences between unruly children and aggressive dogs in unbearable pain reveal themselves in the silence.

Randy's chin dropped down to his chest, and his hand covered his brow. He shook his head, as if answering a question from the floor, and let his tears fall onto the linoleum. His shoulders heaved.

"It's not his fault, Ed . . ."

"I know."

"He's a sweet dog, really. He's only mean because, because . . . he's so afraid."

"I know."

"This . . . isn't . . . fair."

Dr. Ed knew that, too. He knew it the way he knew that somewhere in the city, an old woman was surrendering her cat to the pound, because she couldn't afford to feed it anymore, the way he knew that a dying AIDS patient was handing his dog to a friend and sobbing, because he knew he'd never it see it again, the way he knew that in some abandoned building, a child was watching in tears as an older brother pushed the family dog into a pit fight. He knew it the way he knew that all the sympathy he felt for the hurting all around him couldn't replace not knowing how to heal what hurt.

None of it was fair, but right now, an aggressive dog, a dog who'd have to endure months of additional pain and would never trust people no matter how hard Randy tried, lay in the back room under the X ray machine with the sedative in his blood wearing off.

"Randy?"

Randy's head shot up. "I can't make this kind of decision. I can't. What if I'm *wrong*?" Randy thrust his head back down and stumbled to the back room to be with Louis.

Dr. Ed folded his arms across his chest, walked back to the X ray, and shook his head again. *Euthanasia. From the Greek:* eu meaning *"good" and* thanatos *meaning "death."* Euthanasia was painless, respectful, and distress free. *If the cerebral cortex is rendered nonfunctional by drug depression, no pain is experienced. Rapid loss of consciousness is followed by cardiac arrest and loss of brain function.* That was all, a smooth sail into painless, solitary nothingness. But was it a *good death*? If only he knew more. If only someone hadn't done this to the dog. If only he, Ed, was at home right now, at the dinner table with his wife and kids, and Louis was just another case of heartworm.

From the back room, Randy's sobs filtered in. Dr. Ed looked up at the ceiling, then down at the floor, then up at the ceiling again.

Despite years of practice, he never got used to this part, always expected to expect it somehow, but it crept up on him each time. He felt ambushed by a second-rate thug.

He sighed.

"I need to make this decision for him," he thought. "I have to take this off his shoulders."

Dr. Ed walked out of the examination room and headed for the back of the clinic. The end of another long day.

Randy drove past the warehouse, slowed down but didn't pull in. He hadn't said a word since leaving the clinic, but now he cleared his throat.

"Louis didn't need to die tonight. What he needed was a chance and then a second chance and a third.

"But society doesn't let that sort of thing happen, you know? It's all about raising money and more money and getting your name in the papers, so you can raise even more.

"I bet it's like that with helping people, too. But it's not real. It's just pretending to be real, pretending to be grown up, professional, capable. 'Look at me, I'm raising lots of money. Ain't I a swell and capable guy?' But during all the planning and strategizing, what gets lost? Helping the things that need to be helped."

The bus clattered around the potholes on Chouteau. To the north, lights from downtown St. Louis shone against the cobalt night, like something breathing, like something warm and still alive.

"You know, before Dr. Ed got to the building today, and Louis was all crumpled up in pain, I felt like he was saying, 'Hey, Randy, look at me; I'm *really* fucked up here.' Only I couldn't deal with that, you know? I felt like I had to be the King of Rescue, so I could say to the reporters, 'I have never had to put a dog to sleep,' and then I'd be a hero and then I'd get more money.

"I was pretending. That's not being a hero. Louis was in pain. He was in horrible, horrible pain, and I should have been braver and said to him, 'Hey, Louis, I'm not going to make you suffer anymore.' "

As he pulled in to the neat, brick-lined entrance of Lafayette Square, past the rows of restored gas lamps and refurbished town houses with unbroken windows and televisions glowing inside, he sighed and pulled out a cigarette.

"Someday, maybe we'll get a big grant, and then we can buy a big farm where all of the dogs like Louis can go."

He lit the cigarette.

"That would be so nice."

Chapter Twelve

Saving Hannah

Randy watched the two men saunter across the parking lot toward him, then looked at Peggy Hightower, who sat in her car. She'd been following him on the way to feed several female dogs and their pups when Randy spotted the large yellow-and-white male sniffing at the base of the convenience-store Dumpster and stopped there instead.

A brisk north wind rolled plastic bags, church flyers, want ads, and empty cigarette packs across the cracked asphalt like tumble-weeds, then whisked them up against the store's barred windows with their ads for the state lottery, prepaid phone cards, and Thanksgiving Day specials on white bread and beer.

Like many inner-city neighborhoods, this one had no supermarket—the last one had closed when the chain decided that security costs, among other things, made operations too expensive—so residents without cars or the money for bus fare bought their groceries here instead. Markups on snack crackers, canned meats, cookies, potato chips, hot dogs, packaged popcorn, and soda were tremendous; milk, when there was milk, cost three times as much per gallon as premium gasoline.

A group of men stood in front of the store and watched as the other two walked toward Randy. They eyed the lime-green bus with its dents and its decals and its "Ban Puppy Mills!" sticker and nudged each other and grinned.

"What you doin' here?" one of the men asked.

"Trying to catch a dog."

The man squared his stance, leaned his head back, and viewed Randy from the bottom half of his eyes.

"What?"

Randy nodded toward the Dumpster, where the yellow-and-white dog scratched at the lid of a Styrofoam box. "He's in pretty bad shape."

The two men looked at the dog, who bent his head to bite at the lid of the box. "That's one ugly dog, man. Is it yours?"

"No. It's a stray. Just trying to catch him."

"What for?"

Randy shrugged. "It's what I do."

The two men grinned and nudged each other again. "Man, there's stray dogs all *over* this neighborhood. Give us ten bucks, and we'll show you worse ones than him. Besides, it'll cost you money to park here."

Randy nodded and dug $20 out of his pocket. He always brought tens and twenties when he was out on the streets. "Listen, I'll give you this if you go into the store and buy me some lunch meat."

Both of the men leaned their heads back and stared at Randy suspiciously.

"You can keep the change."

The men turned their heads and stared at him sideways.

"It's for the dog."

Not that he had any business spending $20 on lunch meat for another dog. He didn't have room for any more dogs, and it seemed the more publicity and money and volunteers the group got, the more dogs needed their help. They were everywhere. He was drowning in them. In the shop, at his town house, at foster parents' houses, in his mother's yard, at the kennel, at Dr. Ed's, in his dreams.

Ever since Louis's death, a nightmare on automatic rewind plagued his sleep: he chased a deformed dog through a blazing abandoned building, then through a circus tent, then through a playground, then across a wide-open plain, where it disappeared at the horizon line and over the edge of a cliff.

At that moment, as he waited for the two men to bring him the lunch meat, he had to find an emergency foster home for Dino, who'd been in three foster homes already, and for the two white Shepherd puppies, and for Bear, the monstrous Mastiff mix who tore up any pen he was in, who was now destroying his mother's garage, and who couldn't be taken to adoption days at PetsMart because there'd be no PetsMart left.

But worst of all, worse than the nightmares or Dino or the state of his mother's garage, were Boogie and Spanky, a pair of Bonnie's puppies, just returned to him by the family that had adopted them several years before, when they were puppies. They were too big, the family said, and they climbed on all the furniture and ate them out of house and home and couldn't be controlled and with a new baby on the way . . .

Now Boogie and Spanky—who because of their size and their need to stay together couldn't find a home—sat in a pen in the donated building like two large icons of everything that was wrong. Like everything beyond him. Like everything come undone.

The two men bounced out of the store with a package of honey-cured ham and two six-packs of beer. As Randy unwrapped the meat and headed for the Dumpster, the men settled on the curb and popped open their cans.

The dog was a sturdy Pit Bull mix, but starvation had eaten away at his muscles while mange and festering wounds ate away at his skin. He wasn't neutered, which probably meant he had venereal disease, and by the worn-out look in his eyes, he probably also had heartworm. There was a stub at the base of his spine where his tail used to be—his former owners had wanted less of a target in the fight ring or just thought a docked tail looked cool—he shivered from cold, malnutrition, and nerves, and he limped on three bruised legs. Another all-American dog.

When Randy knelt and held out a slice of ham, the dog's ears went back, his tail stub went down, and he backed away and growled. But it was a tired growl, a burnt-out threat made too many times in vain, and as Randy inched forward and the meat's scent reached him, the dog's brown eyes widened. He trembled all over at the smell.

"Come on, buddy, let's get you out of this place."

Despite his fear, the dog's neck stretched forward until his quivering black nose and whiskers made contact with the meat. Then he snatched it out of Randy's hand, spun around, and ran away.

"Hey, come back. Don't be afraid."

On the curb, the two men leaned into each other and giggled as the dog disappeared down the street.

"Man, we could have told you, you can't catch none of these dogs."

Randy walked back and knelt as he scribbled his phone number on a scrap of paper he grabbed off the pavement.

"Listen, you know what that dog looks like, right? I'll give you twenty bucks if you see him again and call me right away. I'll give you more if you can trap him in a yard or get a rope around him or something, okay?"

The men leaned back, leery, not at all sure that the wrong answer wouldn't set this guy off, and watched him, closely, out of the corners of their eyes.

The industrial beat of Cabaret Voltaire wafted down from the top floor of the town house while Paul got ready for work. Randy sat in a haze of cigarette and calming-candle smoke in front of the television set, watching the Home Shopping Network, his Things-I-Have-to-Do-*Today* list on his lap: *Jo-pregnant-mange-ringworm. Call about adopt-a-thon. Organize all Stray Rescue material. Return calls. Cancel meeting at noon. Call about puppies. Call about fundraiser. Call about Boogie and Spanky. Organize volunteer meeting. Call Dr. Ed about tranquilizers for Bear. Home visit at 7 P.M.*

At his side sat his home phone, his cell phone, a stack of loose notebook paper, an address book, a cup of cold coffee, and an empty box of Twinkies. As the chef on television sliced through a box of frozen peas, Randy grabbed a sheet of paper and scratched down the order number for Ginsu knives.

"It's the only way I can get my Christmas shopping done," he said. "I've already ordered twenty Clappers and ten Chia Pets."

The home phone rang.

"And a vacuum cleaner for my mom."

The phone rang again.

"Hello?"

It was a volunteer who was going away for three weeks, so Randy needed to find another place for the dog she was fostering.

Randy leaned over the calming candle and inhaled deeply. Then he called another volunteer who said he couldn't foster the dog, because he was moving that weekend but promised to call two other families for Randy and let him know right away.

"He's got telemarketing experience," Randy said as he gripped a cigarette in his mouth, winced against the smoke, and finished writing down the order number for the knives. "He's good at helping me find foster homes."

The cell phone rang.

The chef held up both sides of the sliced-through box of peas.

"Hello?"

It was a woman who'd read about Stray Rescue in the newspaper and wanted to help out. As Randy explained the process to her— she'd have to fill out a questionnaire, pass a home visit, and go through some training—the call-waiting beep sounded in his ear, and he put the woman on hold.

"Hello?"

It was a foster parent. The dog Randy had given her was "too rambunctious." He put her on hold, leaned over the calming candle, brushed the smoke toward his face, and clicked back to the new volunteer to tell her he'd call her right back.

He wrote down her phone number. Paul bounced down the stairs and waved from the kitchen. The home phone rang. The chef sawed through a tin can.

"Hullo?"

It was the second volunteer calling back to say he'd found a family who could take the dog but only for a week. Randy put him on hold while he switched to his cell phone and told the woman with the rambunctious dog that he'd come and see her that afternoon.

Paul mouthed a good-bye and walked out the back door. The chef smiled and held up a tomato. Randy lit another cigarette and picked up the home phone as the cell phone rang again.

"Hullo?"

It was a man who said he had a yellow-and-white dog trapped in his backyard.

Peggy went with him. When they pulled up to the place—a soot-splashed, white clapboard house with a caved-in roof, a couch and wringer-washer on the front porch, and Christmas lights coiled around a broken banister—the dog was pacing in the backyard, inside what looked like a former chicken coop.

"That's him, all right," Randy said.

A second dog, a chestnut-brown female with long, flapping ears, a muzzle the size of a car battery, and huge paws with broken toes that curved up at odd angles, emerged from a field next to the house and headed across the yard toward them. She was so heavy with pregnancy that she waddled. Randy tried to ignore her, especially her belly, but she caught his eyes with own urgent gaze, and he looked away too late.

A man, not one of those he'd given his number to at the convenience store, stepped onto the front porch of the house with a box of carryout chicken in his hands.

"Is she your dog?" Randy pointed to the brown female.

The man shook his head as he rooted through the box of chicken. "Naw, she hangs out in the field. But I got that yellow dog penned out back for you."

"How'd you get my number?"

"Friends of mine said you was lookin' for him."

The man led them to the backyard where a flock of crows scattered and squirrels shot up rotting trees. A cat skittered through an open cellar window at the base of the house. The yellow-and-white dog pulled at the side of the wire-mesh pen with his teeth. When he saw the three people watching him, he backed into the corner of the pen and growled.

"He's pretty agitated," Randy said as he pulled a packet of sedatives from his coat pocket. "I'm going to try and drug him, but"— he eyed the box of chicken in the man's hands—"I'll need some really good food to put it in, so he'll eat it."

The man looked at Randy and Peggy and they looked back at him. Then he looked down at the chicken.

"Aw, it's my dinner, man."

Twenty minutes later, sated with sedatives and chicken, the yellow-and-white dog went down. The three of them muzzled him and Randy lugged him back to the bus. The brown female was still sitting there, swishing her tail back and forth in the dirt as if glad her ride had arrived.

Randy stepped past her and laid the male dog in the bus.

"You sure she doesn't belong to someone around here?" he asked hopefully.

"That ugly thing? Look at her toes, man."

Randy covered the male with a blanket as Peggy climbed into the bus, and the female dog, rapt with expectation, stood swishing her tail at his feet.

She was pregnant and unhealthy and had weird toes. Nobody would adopt a pregnant dog who looked like an ill-bred Basset Hound with lanky legs and with toes like the claws of some long-extinct raptor.

And he didn't have room, anyway. Boogie and Spanky, two other undesirables, were in the building right now, and with the new yellow-and-white male, and with Bear, and with a dozen—no, at least two dozen—others whose foster parents were waiting anxiously by their phones for his I-found-a-permanent-home call, because their wards tore up their houses and scared their friends, he couldn't take another one in. He couldn't save them all. As Louis's death had taught him, he shouldn't even try.

But something in the way the brown dog looked up at him seemed familiar, far-off yet hauntingly clear.

Besides, when they walked right up and begged . . .

"Come on," he said. "Get in."

———

The shelter's two rooms were dark, except for the orange glow of the heat lamp in the whelping cage, and as light snow flicked on the roof and Boogie and Spanky rustled in the other room, Christmas music tinkled out of a small portable radio parked on a cardboard box.

"*Siii-lent night. Hooo-ly night . . .*"

In the whelping cage, backlit by the heat lamp, Randy flung the cell phone into mounds of shredded newspaper.

"I don't believe this. I just don't *believe* this."

Among many of the unbelievable matters making themselves at home in his lap this night were Dr. Ed's decision to go out of town for the holidays, the decision of the brown female, now named Hannah, to go into labor on Christmas Eve, and the emergency clinic's refusal to let Randy bring her in.

"They say I have an overdue account of seventy-five dollars from more than a year ago," he said. "I *know* I don't owe them any money. I've been in there like a zillion times in the past year and they never said anything about it."

Curled in the corner of the pen, Hannah stared up at Randy and whimpered. He paced back and forth through the drifts of shredded paper.

"I can't believe this is happening to me. I don't. I told the receptionist or whatever she is that I'd bring a check in, but she said she couldn't process it because she's just filling in for someone else or something. They call themselves an emergency clinic, they call themselves *doctors,* for God's sake . . ."

Hannah whimpered again and jerked her head back toward her tail. Because she was so malnourished and had heartworm and the treatment would complicate her delivery, Dr. Ed told Randy to rush her to the city's emergency clinic, the city's *only* emergency clinic, if she went into labor while he was gone.

"She started acting weird a couple of hours ago, circling around and crying," Randy said. "But now I have no one to call, no one to help me. They told me to, get this, they told me at the emergency clinic to 'let nature take its course.'"

He picked up a blue bulb syringe, then threw it back on the ground. "What am I supposed to do with *that* thing, anyway?"

Hannah bit at the base of her tail. The sides of her body contracted and loose skin rippled over her ribs.

"What is it, Hannah?" Randy bent down and crawled across the paper bedding. "What's wrong? Is something wrong?"

As he bent over Hannah's swelling back end, his eyes widened, his jaws unfurled, and he held the sides of his face as if staring at something awful on a clean kitchen floor.

"*Have a hol-ly-jol-ly Christmas. It's the best time of the year. . . .*"

Hannah's eyes glazed, her ribs shuddered, her skin washed over her ribs like rapids over logs. Randy backed away on his knees.

"Oh my God. Please, don't tell me . . . I think one is coming out. I don't know what to do."

He searched the blackness outside of the cage as if it might hold an instruction manual.

"What am I supposed to do?"

He crawled toward the cell phone on his knees.

"I can't remember. Let nature take its course. Let nature take its course. Jesus, what does *that* mean?"

He looked at the phone shaking in his hand, tried calling the emergency clinic again, then threw it down and crawled back over to Hannah.

"God, please help me. I can't do this. I can't do this."

Hannah groaned, and as her eyes shut and her tail lifted and her body quivered from the effort of the final contraction, the first puppy plunged out onto the newspaper in a slimy, gray bag of mucus.

"Oh, my God. There it is."

Hannah nudged the puppy with her nose, then nibbled at the edges of the bag with the tips of her front teeth.

"*Look.* She knows what to do."

But the tiny, curled figure in the bag didn't move, and as Hannah licked and tugged at the sack of mucus, then pushed it around with her muzzle, then licked and tugged some more, then stood up for a better view and edged it in a small circle with the side of her deformed paw and licked and nipped some more, it still didn't move, and Randy's hands came down slowly from the sides of his face as he leaned and then lunged for the phone and hit redial.

"It's not breathing, for God's sake, *help me* here!" he yelled into the receiver as his eyes stayed pinned to Hannah. "It's just lying there."

Hannah sniffed and circled around her pup.

"Yeah," Randy said, "Uh-huh . . . then I . . . okay . . . then . . . okay . . . okay." With the phone wedged between his shoulder and his ear, he grabbed a towel and the blue bulb syringe. "Uh-huh . . . yeah . . . then what?" He walked on his knees, across the cage toward the puppy and gently pushed Hannah aside. "Okay, I remember now." He snapped the phone shut.

He scooped the puppy up into the towel as Hannah, at his side, whined and shoved her frantic nose under his arms, against his hands, around his knees, and back up under his arms.

"It's okay, it's okay, girl, I remember now. I've got to get it breathing."

Randy rubbed the pink body inside the towel as he had Bonnie's puppies, two of whom now slept orphaned in the other room. Then, with the puppy still wrapped in his hands, he jerked it toward the floor to jar its sinuses clear, then held the blue syringe up to its nostrils and squeezed mucus into the bulb, then rubbed the pup again, then jerked it again, then rubbed and sucked and jerked some more.

The puppy, with its head rolling from side to side on its limp neck, lay in his hands like a cold, wet ball of pink seaweed.

He laid it down on the newspaper and let Hannah sniff at his failure. When she pushed at it with her large nose, the force of the nudge sent it flopping to its other side, and Hannah lay down and curled her body around it. How long would it take before she realized it was dead?

"It's dead, sweetie."

With long, slow licks, Hannah cleaned the body, from its tiny, sealed ear stubs to its comma-shaped tail, and as she worked, as her rough tongue swabbed its fur and scoured its belly, as she shined up its nose and polished its paws, as she prepared it to suckle, prepared it to live, she glanced up at Randy for endorsements.

"You're a good mom."

An hour later, at midnight, as the Westminster Choir began Handel's *Messiah* on the radio, another dead puppy splashed out. *"Every valley shall be exalted . . ."* Twenty minutes later, another dead puppy, then another and another. Randy rubbed and jerked and laid each one at Hannah's side before he eventually pulled it from her sight. *"And His name shall be called"*—she whimpered— *"Wonderful"*—and circled and cried—*"Counsellor"*—and howled after each surrender—*"the mighty God"*—until the next contraction, the next wave, the next chance overwhelmed her.

Around three A.M., long after Randy had thrown the cell phone at the radio, Hannah weakened. She lay on her side panting, laboring for air, as Randy, drenched in sweat, sat hunched next to her and stroked her ears.

"Please, don't die."

He ran his palm down the side of her heaving body. She lifted her head off the ground to see if he wanted anything from her, then let it plop back.

"It's not fair," he whispered. He closed his eyes.

"She doesn't deserve this. It's not her fault, and she shouldn't have to go through this pain."

He opened his eyes and tears beaded at their rims.

"She's been through enough in her life already. All I want for her, for all of them—Bonnie and Louis and Boogie and Spanky and the warehouse pack—is for them to have one good day, just one perfect day in their whole entire, miserable, messed-up lives, when they aren't scared and hungry and in pain. That's all."

He laid his head down on his outstretched arm with his nose close to hers.

"When I was little, I remember I tried to feed some kittens that were in a storm sewer, only I couldn't let my dad know, so I'd stash dinner scraps in my pockets and would sneak out after dark and throw that food down to them. I never saw them, only heard them."

He reached his hand up to Hannah's muzzle and ran his fingers around her nose.

"I understood how scared they were down there. Scared of everything and everybody. Only I remember thinking that I had it so much better than they did. At least I had a house to sleep in, and food. They were as scared of life as I was, but they were so much more *vulnerable*.

"And now, every time I see a dog out there, scared and all messed up, I think about how I felt back then, at night, when I threw food down into that sewer, about how good it made me feel to ease their suffering even for just a few minutes.

"It was the first time I remember feeling truly happy. It's selfish, really, but if I can make them feel safe for just one day, then it makes me feel good, you know, happy, in my heart, and it's only in the company of animals that I feel that way."

Another wave of internal pressure rolled down Hannah's exhausted body. Randy sat up. He wiped his eyes.

"It's like a recipe, really. Everything falls into place to make you who you are. If I hadn't been so afraid of my father, if I hadn't grown up to be so afraid of everything because of him, then I wouldn't feel the way I do about the dogs. And when I think about how many dogs I've helped feel safe, it makes the hell of my child-hood seem somehow . . . *important.*"

The contraction surged across Hannah's ribs, but she didn't lift her head, only panted for air and stared at the wall.

"It's not fair that she has to go through all this pain and not have anything to show for it."

Her muscles urged another puppy down the birth canal, and her hips quivered, and Randy grabbed another towel, and her back end bulged, and another puppy spilled out, and Randy caught it at the end of its slide.

"I've got to get *one* of them breathing for her."

He rubbed the puppy in the towel between his hands, then thrust it down toward the floor.

"Come on, little shit, *breathe.*"

He rubbed and thrust the puppy down again and again and again, until his breath came short, and his face contracted, and sweat flew off him against the warm orange glow of the heat lamp.

He stood up and jerked the puppy harder toward the floor, then lifted it higher and jerked it harder and then . . .

. . . watched it fly out of his hands . . .

. . . and sail across the cage and disappear, as if swallowed, un-der mounds of shredded paper.

He stared down at his empty hands.

"Where'd he go?"

He fell to his knees and waved his hands over the bloody, mucus-laced tendrils of paper as if feeling for body heat from below.

"Where is he?" He spun around on his knees. "Where'd he go?"

He plunged his hands down into the mounds of newspaper and

pushed them back and forth, feeling for the puppy. He grabbed handfuls of paper and threw them behind him, then turned and clutched the same handfuls and threw them somewhere else, and as he flung dirty towels and clean towels and blue bulb syringes into the air, as he tore through the hills and the valleys of the piles of the paper, as the sweat, tinged orange from the heat lamp, streamed down his face—"He *has* to be here *somewhere*"—Hannah's nose, followed by her head, followed by the rest of her pain-racked body, rose up and swayed in place.

She waded out into the shredded-mucky deep and sniffed until she found the familiar smell. She pawed at the top of the paper, then buried her nose and brought her head back up with the puppy balanced between her jaws.

Randy rested on his knees and watched Hannah limp back to the corner with the dead puppy in her mouth. She laid it on the ground and stood over it, licked it and warmed it, calmed its breathless body for reasons she couldn't help. Randy crawled to her side and picked the puppy up in a towel. Transfixed, paralyzed with fatigue, he stared down at the thing in his hands.

With slow, defeated strokes, he rubbed the small dead thing in the towel. Then it sneezed.

He threw open the towel to see one tiny paw flip back and forth in the air.

"It's alive."

He closed the towel back around it and rubbed harder and faster and then stopped when he heard it squeak.

"It's *alive*."

He grabbed a bulb syringe and withdrew mucus from its nostrils. Now when he rubbed it, it let out a minute wail. Hannah's head came up, her ears shot forward, and her nose zeroed in on his hands.

"Look, Hannah." Randy broke into exhausted, overtaxed, almost hysterical laughter and laid the crawling, clawing ball of life at her feet. "This one actually . . . works."

Hannah's tongue enveloped the puppy as Randy, still laughing, bent over and pushed it toward her teats. Its mouth opened when it felt the warm moist skin at its lips; it grabbed hold, and the first milk dribbled down its chin, and Hannah laid her head down and closed her eyes. Randy wiped tears from cheeks.

"We should probably name him Jesus."

By dawn, Hannah's body had pumped out eight more puppies. In all, only four lived. As Randy lay next to them, playing with their back paws while they nursed, Boogie and Spanky, in the other room, woke up and demanded their morning walk.

Hannah waited to develop mastitis until Dr. Ed got back into town. It was two days after Christmas, and Randy, still sleep-deprived, just stared at Dr. Ed after he made the diagnosis.

Dr. Ed shrugged. "Sorry, but that's what it is."

Randy's eyes moved to Hannah, who sat at his feet licking her hot, swollen teats, then to the four puppies squirming in their basket, then back to Dr. Ed.

"I can't . . . I . . . I can't go through that again."

Dr. Ed folded his hands across his chest and nodded at the floor. "I think I heard there's a nursing female at the city pound."

Yes, said the volunteer at the pound, who was also a Stray Rescue volunteer, there was a nursing mother. Yes, the volunteer said, she would come and get the four puppies at the clinic, and yes, she said, Randy would have to find the nursing mother a very good home.

Later, after good-byes had been said to the puppies and the volunteer had whisked the basket away and Randy had tugged at Hannah's leash to go home, Dr. Ed handed him a packet of medicine as if it were something important and holy.

"They're antidepressants." He rolled his eyes down toward Hannah. "I think she'll be needing them."

Back at the Stray Rescue shelter, the lingering scent of puppies drove Hannah mad: she bellowed and howled and tore at the cage, she panted and paced in her confined isolation, she accused Boogie and Spanky with bared fangs and threats. Randy started dialing for favors.

"If you could foster her just for a few days . . . She's freaking out about her . . . Yeah, I understand, but . . . She's depressed and has mastitis, so. . . . She has medicine . . . I understand, but just for a few days, I swear, just until . . . Uh, I don't know why the medicine isn't working, but . . . Just a little whining . . . Look, the truth is, I can't stand to see her this way, okay? I feel like I've ripped out her heart with my own bare hands."

When Hannah walked through the front door of her new foster home, she set out to find her pups. She tore through the house, through the dirty laundry basket, through the garbage cans and bookcases, in and out of every room, under every chair, and under every bed. Later, left alone in the house for a few hours, she tore down miniblinds, pulled clothes off hangers, gouged toenail marks in doors, and cracked a plate-glass window.

That night, she whimpered and paced incessantly. Whenever she heard something—a howling cat, a distant car alarm, a muffled cough—anything that *might* be them, her whimpering sailed into a full-blown howl. She was back in the shelter the next day.

"I can't stand it, I mean, look at her," Randy said as he sat cross-legged in the doorway between the two rooms and stared into Hannah's cage. He'd doubled her medication, which made her sullen and groggy, but she sat, eyes drooping, ears sagging, heart slowing, and fought it off, afraid to fall alone into sleep.

Behind Randy, Boogie and Spanky wrestled in their cage. "And what am I going to do about *them*?"

Since Paul was out of town, Randy brought Hannah to the town house that night and doubled his own medication so he could sleep through her tortured pacing. In the morning, she clung to his side, got underfoot, and growled when the other dogs came near him. She attached herself to the only constant thing she knew besides the gnawing aloneness.

Over the next few days, her behavior worsened. "It's like she's possessed," Randy said. She peed in the house, terrorized the other dogs, refused to eat, chewed on the rugs, monopolized the furniture, and shredded the mail as it slid in through the slot. When Randy left the town house, he could hear her howling two blocks away, and when he returned, she greeted him by skidding across the wood floor and slamming her eighty-pound body into him.

But during the first weeks of the New Year, Hannah accepted the solidity of her new life, basked in her new pack, and as she found a role in the new family unit, the memory of the puppies lost its grip.

Meanwhile, dozens of other dogs came and left the Stray Rescue building while Boogie and Spanky, still big, still inseparable, still orphaned, watched them come and go. As Randy's fear that no one would ever adopt them threatened to crest, the call came in: a family, with a house and a yard and a fence, was interested—only *interested*—in adopting the two outcast brothers.

Could they "try them out" for a week first?

"Of course."

And could they bring them back if it "didn't work out"?

"No problem," Randy said as he dropped the pair off at their new home. "But everything works out in the end."

Before he left, Randy stood beside the bus and watched Boogie and Spanky slobbering up their new front window. Despite all the time that had passed and all that had changed, he saw Bonnie's face in the window instead. He always had.

And someday, all the dogs he picked up would have homes and become docile, housebroken, paper-fetching pets. Someday all of the flea-bitten evolutionary throwbacks would be chewing on slippers, begging at dinner tables, and barking at doorbells. They'd have squeaky toys, rubber bones, doggy sweaters, designer leashes, gourmet treats, and rawhides. They'd chase Frisbees and ride in cars. They'd become part of the human pack.

Randy saluted the pair at the window and hopped into the bus. During the drive home, his decision to keep Hannah as his own came wrapped in the certainty that while things always worked out, there was never really an end.

Stray

Pack of strays

J. B.

Stray

Pack of strays

M. R.

M. R.

Two strays

Stray

M. R.

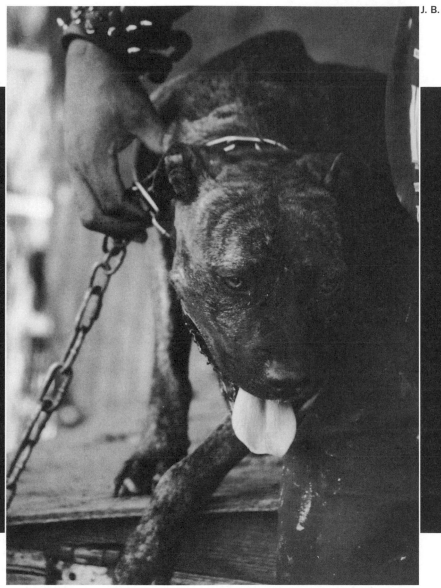

Guard dog

Part Three

Chapter Thirteen

A Pack Divided

Randy sat on the tire rim watching Lester toss pieces of kibble into an empty coffee can over the small fire they shared. Outside, night wind rattled the warehouse; inside, restless pigeons shifted in the rafters. Thick deposits of feathers littered the floor around them, and Randy wondered out loud if the birds were molting.

Lester shrugged and leaned closer to the fire. Deep lines ran down his whiskered face like grooves of erosion down a sandbank, and his eyes, rheumy and dull, seemed to have trouble focusing.

"Have you seen Compton?" Randy asked.

The old man shrugged again as the fire popped an ember onto the dirt.

"What about Taz?"

Lester sighed, leaned back on his elbows, and looked for an answer in the rafters. Winter had taken its toll on him. Over the dark months he had grown more and more incoherent, more and more centered on the mathematical symbols he drew in the dirt and on the conspiracy of rats and pigeons he said were unhappy serfs intent on having his head.

The weather had also dealt blows to the pack. After Katlin's rescue in the fall, the group disappeared for several weeks; when it returned, it was thinner and weaker than before, and Taz, the sentry, was missing. Randy checked the usual places—the shelters, the railroad yards, the ditches—but he never saw Taz alone or running with any of the other scattered packs. If he had died, Randy never found his body.

Meanwhile, Compton's sway over the remaining group members deteriorated. When Randy tossed braunschweiger toward them, Sunny, Midnight, and Bashful surged forward while Compton hung back and waited. And when the arthritic leader later stood up to leave, the others hesitated: a clear rejection of his authority.

Without strong leadership, the pack was doomed, but Randy still didn't set traps. "They're not ready," he said, in a tone that suggested his evasion of this final step.

The pack disappeared again after Christmas. When it came back to the warehouse during a snowstorm weeks later, Compton wasn't with them. Randy, with waning energy, searched the usual places.

But a new member had joined the group, a large male Malamute whose purebred lines and subordinate grins, tail wags, and play bows marked him as an abandoned or loose pet. With the two top males gone, the group roamed less, and the Malamute, still strong and untroubled by starvation or disease, adopted Sunny as his mate, while Midnight, ever weakening, fell to the bottom of the dwindling pack.

Bashful inherited the alpha position, but he ruled as awkwardly as a teenage dauphin. Where Compton had negotiated a tenuous truce whenever Randy entered the warehouse, Bashful wagged his tail like a puppy and joined the others in a democratic greeting. Compton had always eaten first, but now when Randy threw out bits of braunschweiger, Bashful joined the lawless, collective scramble for the small treasures and made a tail-down retreat when Sunny growled his way.

Compton had cinched his authority with the emotional distance he kept from the others, which allowed him to enforce the pecking order, but Bashful didn't like being separate. When the Malamute sent Midnight cowering to the ground, the new leader turned his eyes away.

Bashful was also physically weak, and while his street smarts were more honed than those of the inexperienced Malamute, it wouldn't be long before he joined Midnight on the ground.

Randy stared across the fire at Lester's lined face, still tilted up toward the rafters. Around them, the dogs slept at the far edges of the firelight. He knew he had to set traps for them soon, had known it when Taz disappeared, but the warehouse, the late-night fires, the company of the dogs and the crazy old man, provided a convenient hidden shelter for his own fears.

"Chicken," Lester said still gazing at the ceiling. "They taste just like chicken."

Randy followed the old man's gaze up to the rafters, where the pigeons' bow-shaped bellies lined up like the hulls of dark boats at a dock. His eyes dropped to the feathers scattered on the ground.

Lester had been eating the birds.

"You should go to the shelter," Randy said.

Lester grinned and spat into the flames.

Randy and Janet sat in the bus. Through a haze of cigarette smoke, they watched sparrows, starlings, and crows pick at the braunschweiger smeared inside two wire cages in the warehouse yard. The birds had been at it for an hour and at this rate they would eat all the food before Bashful and Midnight, who were asleep in the warehouse, even knew it was there.

In the rail yard behind the Quonset huts, cold mist wafted off the tracks as a man in patched coats picked up beer cans and shoved them into a white plastic garbage bag. Half a mile down, Sunny and the Malamute chased imaginary prey in and around parked trains.

Randy's decision to set the traps that day had come in two installments, the first that morning when he bolted from a dream about Lester eating dogs, the second when his mother told him that her brother—an uncle Randy barely knew—was dying of emphysema and was moving from his home in Florida to a hospital in Missouri to be near her at the end.

"And I want you to quit smoking," she said.

"Please, Mom, not now . . ."

"Promise me you'll quit smoking."

"Mom . . ."

She clutched the sleeve of his robe. *"Promise me."*

"Okay, okay, after today is over, I promise."

Randy, still deep within the dream, stored away his mother's announcement about his uncle like an unopened bill that he would get to along with all the others when he had time. But the talk of death and the look on his mother's face joined the image of a dog on a roasting spit throughout his next cup of coffee, and he picked up the phone and called Janet.

"Randy?"

He looked across the bus toward her. "Yeah?"

"I have to go to the bathroom."

Randy shrugged. "Go in back of the warehouse."

"I can't."

"Lester does."

Janet rolled her eyes. "Nothing has happened in over an hour. I'll be back in fifteen minutes, I promise."

As he watched her trudge toward her SUV in his rearview mirror, two men pushed their shopping carts through the potholes and the mist on the street. Lester was gone, off to wherever it was he went during the day, and Sunny and the Malamute were now specks on the gauzy steel-gray horizon. He slid out of the bus and walked into the warehouse to check on Midnight and Bashful.

"Hey, guys."

Jarred from sleep, Midnight jumped up from the ground, tucked his tail, and skittered out the door past Randy while Bashful sat on Lester's bed and thumped his tail up and down on the sleeping bags.

"How am I going to trap you if you're in here sleeping?"

The tempo of Bashful's tail quickened, but he swiveled his ears back and forth as if not sure where his sentiments rested. He was a lanky dog, dark brown and shaggy, and as he sat there, head cocked, ears forward and then back, tongue draped down from the side of his mouth, Randy swung an arm in a low arc to wave him off the bed.

"You've got mange. Lester doesn't need that on top of everything else."

Bashful lumbered down, ears back.

Then, out in the yard, a quick cold snap of metal on metal. Then a yelp. Randy and Bashful shot looks at the open door, back at each other, then to the open door again.

"Midnight."

The small black Chow, bent forward on his shoulders, scratched and clawed at the ground from inside the bars of the trap. Randy vaulted across the frost-dried weeds. He didn't want Bashful to see Midnight in the cage, so he bear-hugged the trap without greeting its captive and hauled it across the yard to the bus.

He grabbed the bag of braunschweiger from the front seat and dropped bits of meat from the door of the second trap across the yard to the warehouse. He whistled for Bashful and then trotted back to the bus, where Midnight whimpered and cowered in the corner of his cage. Randy stacked bags of dog food next to him, sat down, and pushed his fingers through the bars to stroke Midnight's forehead. His head quivered.

"I'm sorry we had to do it this way."

From the back of the bus, he couldn't see the warehouse doors, but through the bottom half of the bus's front window, he watched the trap. Four starlings landed on it and eyed the braunschweiger through the bars.

"Just hang in there, boy."

Three pigeons flew out of a Quonset hut, landed, and circled the trap. Under Randy's fingers, Midnight trembled.

The birds turned their heads in unison toward the warehouse and then sprang into flight as Bashful, nose to the ground, appeared in the front window of the bus.

"Here he comes, Midnight. It's working. Hang in there, boy."

Following the meat, Bashful inched across the weeds toward the open door of the trap. He sniffed inside, then raised his head and searched the yard, then sniffed inside the cage again. He stretched his neck forward, nose volleying from side to side as if yanked by a string, and when his front paw stepped into the trap, Randy scrambled across the floor of the bus to the base of the two front seats. Rising from a crouch, he lifted his body until his eyes met the horizon of the dashboard.

Outside, Bashful sensed movement in the bus and jerked his front leg out of the trap. He turned and looked across the yard, and Randy froze on half-bent knees. Bashful waved his nose back and forth in the air, but all it caught was the smell of the meat, and he turned and stepped back inside the trap. When the door snapped down behind him, he scuttled forward, spun around, and like Midnight, burrowed for an exit.

"*Yes.*"

Randy clawed his way up and over the passenger seat and flung the door open wide.

Over the next weeks, Midnight and Bashful recuperated at Dr. Ed's clinic, and Stray Rescue volunteers readied the new building with donated heating, air-conditioning, telephones, a roof, a washer and dryer, a state-of-the-art computer system, and well-lit kennels—apartments, Randy called them—for up to twenty dogs. As Randy filled the building with new strays, his uncle Albert was flown from Florida to a hospital in St. Louis.

He also went back to the warehouse every day, but, as if they understood what had happened to their pack mates, Sunny and the Malamute had disappeared. By the time Midnight and Bashful moved from the clinic to the new building, Lester was gone again, too.

Randy placed Midnight and Bashful in one of the apartments together. At first, the sight of people sent the duo slinking to the corners, where they faced the wall, hunched their backs, and convulsed with shudders; not even braunschweiger accompanied by song could coax them out.

Because he didn't want any of the dogs in the building to attach themselves to just one person, which would happen when hunger and the need to belong drew them out, Randy set up a round-robin. Volunteers came to the building at least four times a day, and after reading the dogs' charts—"Needs one white pill at 8 A.M."; "Has heartworm, no strenuous exercise"; "Needs two blue pills at noon for eye infection"; "Doesn't walk on leash well yet"; "Two droppers of pink medicine at night in food"; "Has mange, use gloves"; "Sweet temperament but scared and just had chemo treatment so acting a little weird"—they fed, medicated, talked to, played with, and when they could, walked all of the dogs in the building.

It didn't take more than a few weeks for most of the dogs to learn that people wouldn't hurt them, wouldn't lash out or take them by surprise. When they were ready, they were sent to foster homes, where they learned how to sleep on sofas, play with children, chew rawhide, and navigate stairs. They acclimated themselves to regular feedings, baths, and trips to the vet. They learned to recognize the sound of certain footsteps, certain cars. They relaxed. When they were ready for the next step, when they didn't fear-bite or circle in corners or cry in their sleep anymore, they were ready to go to permanent homes.

For Midnight and Bashful, the trip home was slow. Both were feral and had survived longer within the safe borders of a pack than had their stray counterparts alone on the streets. After several months, Bashful still clung to the corners of his kennel, denying eye contact. But Midnight pranced in place and whimpered with excitement when Randy or a volunteer came in.

It was a blow when Randy realized that Midnight was ready to leave, but after he chose the perfect foster family—a couple with a house in the suburbs—and coaxed Midnight into their car and watched them drive away, he found the blows had just begun.

The call came later that day. Midnight's foster parents, sharing the phone and crying so that Randy could barely understand them, said that Midnight had run away.

"He ran *away*?"

When they got home, they put Midnight inside the house, then went back to the car to get something they forgot. He nudged the screen door open and took off.

"Took *off*?"

He took off down the street, they said, and they hadn't seen him since.

Randy pushed the bus across the city as fast as it would go. When he reached Midnight's foster home, deep in the suburbs, he jumped out of the bus, rushed to the door, then searched the front yard, the backyard, and every room, hoping that his mind merely had played some maladjusted trick. He walked the smooth, unfamiliar streets, and when it turned dark, he got a flashlight out of the bus and called Janet on his cell phone.

They searched for hours. They tiptoed over fresh-swabbed driveways, through well-lit park paths, down empty streets named after English ports and dead poets. They maneuvered in silence around unlocked bicycles, unchained snow blowers, and unfettered barbecue grills. There were no Dumpsters to look behind, no railroad tracks to follow, no empty buildings or littered fields to walk through. There were no police sirens or car alarms or crosstown buses, and every time they called Midnight's name through the darkness, it was as if an air-raid siren had gone off.

"He'll die out here," Randy whispered as they whisked their flashlights across boxwood and frozen azaleas. "There's nothing here for him, no food, no place to hide, nothing."

A calico cat, backlit by the blue glow of a TV, stared at them from inside a bay window.

"Maybe," Janet said, "he's headed back to the warehouse."

Randy pounced on the suggestion and carried it with him for the next several weeks. Every morning he checked the warehouse, checked the railroad yard, checked the alleys up and down. He tore through every shelter, every pack haunt, every lost-and-found page of every newspaper he could find. And in the afternoons—because Lester wasn't around to build fires—he sat in the empty warehouse and cried.

"I killed him. *I* killed him. I'm as guilty as if I'd strangled him myself. I should have never trapped him like that. He just wasn't . . . ready."

He put up flyers and pounded on strange doors, but all he

got for his efforts were calls and sad stories about other stray dogs. While searching, he found two new packs and a litter of puppies under a bridge, and he stole a starving female dog from the yard where she was chained.

One afternoon, while driving through a stretch of truck yards and prefabricated storage sheds, through grimy snow under a matte sky, Randy spotted four dogs trotting single file along a battered chain-link fence. One of them, the one at the rear, looked familiar.

He pulled over, let the engine idle, and watched the group as it followed the line of the fence. They were all unneutered males. The lead dog's ears were forward, his tail was high, and his head moved confidently from side to side as if challenging the weather or the street itself to a fight. The next two jogged close behind him, with their tails hung but not tucked.

The last dog, the low dog, with his ears laid back and his tail wedged between his back legs, followed at a subordinate distance and crouched down when the others looked back.

His body was so ravaged and his posture so changed that it took Randy several moments of squinting against the glare to recognize him.

He jumped out of the bus without grabbing any food or turning off the engine and ran down the street, against the wind and cold and the glare of the snow, calling Compton's name.

Chapter Fourteen

All the Way Home

Randy stared at the lights on the machines, the chrome bedrails, his mother's tears as they spilled onto the floor—at anything but his uncle Albert's heaving chest. The doctor had assured them that once the respirator was turned off, he'd die quickly, but thirty minutes later, his brain was still ordering his lungs to find air.

Nurses padded in and out of the room; benign and distant voices conveyed messages over an intercom. An elevator bell pinged in the hallway. In the corner of the room, shards of crisp morning sun slid in through the blinds and onto the bowed head of his mother who cried, silently, into her hands.

Randy asked her whether she was okay. She nodded into her palms. There was nothing to do and nothing to say—no future plans, no good jokes, no family gossip that mattered anymore.

His uncle gasped and shuddered. Silence followed like a long parade. He gasped again, and the silence lasted longer. This is how it ended. A tortured final turn at the bend followed by a long, last stretch going nowhere.

Randy let his eyes rest on his uncle's face. They'd never been close, but with one easy nod of his head to the doctor, *Yes, go ahead, kill him,* Randy was now on more intimate terms with his uncle than he'd ever been with anyone in his life. He had to say something.

"Did I tell you about the dogs?"

Tell him anything.

"About that pack of dogs in the warehouse?"

Say anything that his uncle could carry with him to wherever it was he was going.

"When I first found them, they were living in this abandoned building with this crazy old man named Lester. . . ."

Randy told him about the gang, about Compton's fear of losing control, about Sunshine's watery brown eyes, about the raves and the pigeons and the old men and their shopping carts. He told him how strange and peaceful a dirty, gray building could be and how he didn't hate Lester anymore.

"I saved Noel first . . ."

He told Albert about rescuing Noel, Sunshine, and Katlin and described the intricacies of their new lives: Noel lived with a family in Kansas City, Sunshine with the symphony conductor, Katlin with a couple who treated her like their child.

He explained how he trapped Bashful and Midnight, omitting the details of Midnight's escape, and then ventured into theories about why Taz and Compton disappeared and never came back.

"Maybe Bashful challenged them for top spot and won, even though that doesn't seem likely. . . ."

He edited his concerns about pain and death and focused instead on the natural order of things, on how the pack members were survivors, on how Bashful would one day develop into a pet, on how Compton had found a new pack.

"I ran after him when I saw him, and he knew who I was. . . . I was running after him, I was calling his name, and even though the other dogs ran like crazy, Compton stopped and looked back at me. He recognized my voice.

"The dogs in front escaped through this hole in the fence, and when Compton saw them running away on the other side, he tried to follow through the hole too, only he got stuck, and I was so relieved to see him, I didn't think about what I was doing, and I grabbed, just grabbed him from behind.

"It scared him, I guess. I mean, I'd never touched him before . . . and he turned around and tried to bite me. I let go, and he slid through the hole after the others . . . and I haven't seen him since.

"But I'll keep looking."

Randy told his uncle about how Lester had disappeared, and about how he looked for him on the streets, just the way he looked for the dogs, but never found him. Then he told his uncle about the day he found Sunny and the Malamute back at the warehouse and how that very morning he'd asked Janet, Mindy, and Ellie to set the traps and how at this moment, the last two pack members might already have been rescued.

"Things always work out in the . . ."

He didn't finish the sentence, just watched his uncle's chest rise and then rest. Rise and then rest. Why had this man traveled from a Florida summer to a Midwest winter to die like a fish on a dock? What made him leave the ocean and the sun and sand in his shoes, his dream, what he'd worked and saved for all his life, and come to an antiseptic hospital room where the view of a slushy city street was the last thing he'd ever see?

In the corner, the sun shifted from his mother's bent head to her shaking shoulders.

He would be a better son. He would quit smoking and eat more regularly and make sure flowers were delivered on her birthday. None of this was his mother's fault—not her brother's imminent death, not her son's phobias, not the crimes of the mind that over-whelmed her husband when he returned from Vietnam—yet she accepted it all like a sentence she deserved. She always had. This and more, which was probably why his uncle wanted her to be the last thing he ever saw.

Randy looked back down at the bed. Gasp. Silence. Gasp. Silence.

"I just realized," Randy said. "I never named the Malamute."

Later that afternoon, Randy left the hospital, steered down Chou-teau toward the warehouse, and begged God for something good, any little scrap He could spare. He forced himself to think about the successes, about Bonnie and the puppy mill dogs and Hannah, but it was hard to think about the dogs when he'd just superin-tended the death of another man.

He punched a cassette into the tape deck and wallowed in mel-odramatic Italian arias, seeking and dutifully finding every sad thing that had ever happened to him in his life.

The bus bounced through deep wounds in the road.

He was sobbing when he pulled into the warehouse yard, and he nearly rammed Mindy's BMW.

His first impression of the scrambling bodies and flailing arms and legs by the side of the Quonset huts was that of a disturbed ant colony. He wiped his face and jumped out of the bus. Mindy, Ellie, and Janet were running in circles around one of the traps, and the Malamute was howling up at the sky in the middle of the yard, and an old man with his shopping cart stood laughing by the fence. Randy's second supposition was that he had stumbled into a fren-zied coven meeting on some very high holy day.

"What's going on?" Randy directed the question to the wailing Malamute.

"Randy!"

He couldn't tell who had called out to him.

"In the trap!"

Mindy was tugging at his coat sleeve.

"We caught . . . Look!"

Ellie's head bobbed up and down.

". . . In the yard!"

Janet waved toward the trap as the old man yelled out incoherent cheers from the street and the Malamute wailed in the weeds.

Randy pushed his way through Mindy, Ellie, and Janet and saw Sunny wincing in the corner of the cage with her head turned away from the noise and her ears flat against her skull. A shudder surged through her matted golden body, and he knelt beside her.

"Sunny."

When he whispered her name, she turned her face toward him and locked her sunken brown eyes onto his. The sound of the three women, the old man, the howling Malamute, his mother's cries, his uncle's heaving chest, Compton's last look back, all faded into the background for that one second, that one fraction of time, when he and Sunny made eye contact and her ears twitched forward and her eyes rounded and it was just the two of them connected and alone in the whole wide world. Seraphim could have landed at that moment and not have inspired him more.

"Randy?"

Sunny shoved her head back into the corner.

"Randy?"

"Huh?"

"What are we going to do about the Malamute?"

Randy pulled himself away from the back of Sunny's head, stood up, and turned toward the howling black-and-white dog in the yard.

"His name is Albert," Randy said.

The Malamute stretched his head back, closed his eyes, rounded his lips, and moaned up to the sky. He was Sunny's mate, and he'd seen Midnight and Bashful taken away in the same trap. He didn't want to be alone; his howl, a knowing, desperate lament, was a way of keeping contact with Sunny for a few last awful minutes.

If Randy put Sunny in the bus now and drove away, Albert would chase them for as long as he could.

Randy wrapped his fingers around the top of Sunny's cage and walked to the bus with its heavy, uneven weight banging against his knees. He apologized to Sunny the whole way, and as he passed Albert, the Malamute stopped howling and stared across the yard. His mate was close to him now, and his ears went forward and his tail wagged as he whimpered to her across the dry, brittle grass.

Randy shoved the cage into the back of the bus but left the doors open. He motioned for Mindy, Ellie, and Janet to hide behind Mindy's car while he hunched down in the shadow of the warehouse.

For the next several minutes, Albert, silent for the first time since Sunny's capture, eyed the car, then the bus, then the warehouse. When the yard seemed abandoned for good, he inched forward, low to the ground, and when he heard Sunny whimper from inside the bus, he straightened and circled the bus at a fast, tail-up, ears-forward trot.

"Go on," Randy whispered as the muscles in his legs tightened underneath him.

Albert stopped by the bus's open back doors and extended his neck inside, nose twitching.

"God, please make him go in."

The Malamute backed away and sat down, cocked his head and yelped in confusion. Across the yard, the old man on the street pushed his nose through the holes in the chain-link fence.

Albert stood up and stepped forward. His head disappeared inside the bus. Then, as he made nose-to-nose contact with Sunny through the bars of her cage, his back end wagged wildly. Then he crouched down. Then he leaped inside.

Randy sprang forward and raced across the yard. He ran fast, faster than when he'd chased Noel through the snowstorm, faster than when he'd first heard Lester's voice from the bowels of the Quonset hut, faster than when he'd chased Compton down the street, faster than in his dreams, faster than time, and when he reached the bus, and he saw the glow of Albert's eyes in the darkness, and he felt his heart beat in his head and the cold metal of the bus's door underneath his hands, and the faces of Noel, Compton, Sunshine, Midnight, Bashful, and Taz swam in his eyes, he slammed the back doors shut. And it was over.

Chapter Fifteen

Grim's Feral Tails

It was nine A.M., and already the sun's rays were taking aim at the pavement, as bright and sharp as thrown knives. In yards the size of phone booth floors, humidity dripped from ornamental wrought-iron fences down onto mossy brickwork and withered ivy. Buses wheezed through the heat up the cobblestones.

Inside the refrigerated town house, Randy pulled down the blinds and threw a Xanax into his mouth, the second one that morning.

"I hate this," he said.

Paul, on the couch, shrugged. "Then why'd you agree to do it?"

Randy turned away from the window and rolled his eyes toward the ceiling as if asking the flat plaster the same question.

"I don't know. I don't know."

"For the dogs," Paul said.

Randy nodded. He wore hiking boots with white socks folded over their upper edges, white shorts, a black tank top under an orange-and-white flowered shirt, narrow yellow-tinted glasses, and an orange bandanna twisted around his head. It was the "rescue outfit" that he wore for the media, and he asked for the fourth time whether it made him look thin.

Hannah followed him as he smoked and brushed dog hair off his shirt and trekked back and forth across the wood floors. He pulled another Xanax out of the front pocket of his shorts and stared at it in the palm of his hand. The telephone rang.

"Hello? That's okay, I'll be here."

Hannah backed away from Randy as he hung up the phone, wagged her tail when he looked her way.

"She'll be here in fifteen minutes. God."

A producer from Animal Planet's *Wild Rescues* had seen the St. Louis puppy-mill rescue story. When she called Randy to ask whether she and her crew could fly to St. Louis and film him rescuing wild dogs for the show, Randy mumbled that it wasn't really all that exciting, that they weren't all wild, that some of the places he went to weren't all that nice, and that predicting the outcome of a rescue was impossible. When he blurted out the real reason— "Cameras scare me"—she laughed and insisted, patiently, like a physician closing in with a needle, that it wouldn't be all that bad.

"You don't understand," he said.

She laughed again and set the date and now she was lost in a rental car in the city but was heading his way.

"What if I make a fool of myself on you-know-what [the phrase "national TV" was banned in the town house that week], I mean, if I sweat—look, I'm sweating already and it's sixty degrees in here—if I fall over something or, or, or what if she asks me a, a, a question and I go blank? I need a drink. Paul, what can you make that seems like breakfast?"

"Baileys and coffee?"

"Make it strong."

They drove—the bus followed by the producer's rental car followed by the Blazer of a local sound and camera crew—across the Poplar

Street Bridge, beyond the shadow of the Arch, over the gray tarmac of the river fringed with casino boats and a floating McDonald's, past billboards advertising strip clubs and late-night rock-and-roll bars, toward Washington Park on the East Side.

"I hate driving on bridges," Randy said.

They drove past vast, empty acres of stockyards and steel mills. They crossed train tracks speared with chickweed and wound around box springs in the road. A field piled with wood pallets, refrigerators, water-heater tanks, and soot-edged sunflowers. A pawn shop. Three yellow-and-brown dogs and a puppy. A burned-out church. An old school with swingless swing sets in the yard.

Randy was taking the film crew to an abandoned house where he'd been feeding a wild mother and her puppy. On the way: junk-yards of gutted train cars; two black puppies hiding under a trailer with their mother; apartments with no doors, houses with no windows, yards with no grass, stores with no glass; Chows and Rottweilers chained to truck tires; children running through primary forests where ice cream shops, grocery stores, and houses once stood and where Pit Bulls, alone and in groups, lounged with Akitas and Dobermans in the dense, leafy shade.

They drove down a street where trailers hollowed by fire sat on lots asphyxiated by cottonwoods, torched cars, faceless television sets, cribs, rotting couches, and stacks of tires, where the charred roofs of three-sided houses folded into the open kitchens and living rooms and dens, where weeds grew from fissures in the road, and where mange-eaten dogs limped down the middle of the street. Old women on porches fanned themselves and eyed the trio of vehicles like villagers watching the occupiers' tanks roll by.

Randy parked the bus, followed by the rental car and the Blazer, in front of a small house with "STAY OUT!" spray-painted in red across its dingy white clapboards. The windows had no panes, the walls tilted inward under the caving-in roof, and the front door hung on one hinge. On the porch, two fan-backed metal chairs sat surrounded by mud, tree branches, railroad ties, and smashed-down cardboard boxes like kindling set out under a pyre.

Tall sycamores shaded the dirt yard, edged with wild strawberries. Past the strawberries stood waist-high grass and the pulsating webs of banana spiders.

He rested his hand on the door handle but stayed in his seat. In the rearview, he watched the producer with her pad of paper, the photographer with his camera, and the sound man with his poles and batteries and microphones get out of their cars.

"I can't do this."

Randy watched Paul, who'd ridden in the producer's car, walk along his side of the bus.

"I can't do this."

Randy wiped his forehead and yanked a cigarette out of his shirt pocket. The producer walked up, her eyebrows arched above her blue-tinted sunglasses.

"I'm sweating," Randy said to Paul through the window.

"Everyone's sweating, so what?"

"You don't care. You're thin and look like a Baldwin brother, and you don't have to run around sweating, chasing dogs, and sounding intelligent on you-know-what."

"Randy . . ."

"I can't do this. I might as well put a rope around my neck right now."

"Randy . . ."

"I should just tell them I'm a fake and get it over with."

"You're not a fake. This what you do. This *is* you."

"I want to hide."

Randy turned and looked through the window at the producer.

The photographer stood beside her and then leaned the lens forward toward the bus window. Randy smiled and held up his index finger. Then dove to the back of the bus.

The sound man peered in at him from the back window. Randy held up his index finger again and rummaged through the snares and dog-food cans and bite gloves and Sonic Burger wrappers as if looking for something vital. Sweat dripped down his nose, trickled across his chest, and seeped through his shirt.

He looked up. They were going to film not a rescue of feral dogs but a self-imposed hostage situation staged by a sweating, drug-crazed coward in the back of an old green bus.

He flipped a stack of papers over his shoulder to give his search a sense of legitimacy and the camera lens something else to stare at, and just then a small black streak caught his eye through the window.

The tail of the puppy he'd been trying to catch for weeks disappeared into the field. He pushed his gaze past the producer to where the puppy's mother stared at the bus across the tops of the weeds.

Randy grabbed a snare and jumped out of the bus.

The chase adhered strictly to the rules of chaos: Paul and the producer waved their arms at the edge of the field; the mother dog, pursued by the photographer, leaped out of the field and slipped under the house; Randy, pursued by the sound man, belly-flopped for the puppy in the weeds. Children, some on mangled bikes, some with no shoes, gathered and hooted on the sidelines.

The puppy bolted the field, its black eyes wide, and raced past Paul and the producer to the back of the house, its stumpy legs pumping at full throttle. Randy waded through the weeds and emerged from the field with dirt, grass, and spiderwebs plastered to his sweaty face.

"They're in the house!" Paul said.

Randy, the producer, and the photographer ran to the back porch buried in shade and in through a dark open door. Inside, the smell of mud. Dozens of television sets with their screens smashed out. Upended, waterlogged couches. Tongues of pink-and-white-flowered wallpaper peeling off gouged-out, plaster-slabbed walls. Black plastic bags of garbage. Holes in the floor. A two-year-old calendar. Empty bottles of beer.

"Trash collection isn't regular here," Randy said to the producer, "so people have to dump stuff where they can. That's why you see so many fires; they're trying to burn their garbage."

Randy stepped over a fallen chunk of ceiling and his foot went through the rotted wood floor. A scurrying in the front room. Paul, still outside, called Randy's name.

"They're in the field again!"

They chased the mother and puppy through the field, herded them back toward the house, and lost them to a hole in the foundation that led to the pitch-dark cellar. Randy, out of breath, stared at the base of the house.

"I'm really sorry about this, but it's almost impossible to catch a dog that doesn't want to be caught." The producer scribbled on her notepad and the camera made faint whirring sounds in his face. "What we tried to do today only terrified them."

His voice cracked and he turned away from the camera. "I'm sorry."

The producer looked up from her pad and smiled. "Come on, let's take a walk."

They strolled away from the house and the photographer and the sound man. When they reached the end of the road, they turned and walked back.

The producer knew what she was doing: giving Randy a few minutes to walk a familiar street, talk about familiar subjects, and face familiar fears. When they reached the house again, Randy smiled at the photographer and cameraman as he fingered the bottom of his shirt. "Okay. I'm sane now."

In the segment that later aired on national television, Randy explained that while the mother dog might have spent some portion of her life as a pet, she'd been on the streets a long time defending herself, scavenging for food, trying to feed and protect her puppies. Now she and her surviving pup followed the surest path to survival, which pointed in the opposite direction of humans. He said that he'd set a trap for them eventually if he had to, but the best way to rescue them was through patient coaxing.

While he talked, a long, white car pulled onto the road and screeched to a stop behind them. On a porch, a woman called a small child off the street. Then the car lurched forward, squealed sideways, and a man in the passenger seat hung his head out the window. "You got no business here," he yelled. "*Go home.*" And the car sped away.

The bus roared west toward the bridge with the rental car and Blazer in its shadow. Randy decided to take the crew to the railroad yards behind the warehouse; with the help of several railroad employees, he was taking care of a new pack there.

Randy checked the rearview mirror as muffled music reached him. "I think we have company," he said, and stopped at the corner.

A low Oldsmobile pulled up alongside the bus. From inside, three young men surveyed the green bus with mild amusement. Randy rolled down his window, and the man on the passenger side leaned out.

"You straight?"

Randy nodded. "Yeah, just looking for some dogs."

The man's eyebrows closed in over the bridge of his nose. "You what?"

"I, uh, run a rescue operation over in St. Louis, and I'm just looking for dogs. I come here all the time. That's a film crew in back of me."

"Hey," a man in the backseat yelled out, his eyes wide with recognition, "you that dog guy?"

"That's me."

The man in the front nodded his head slowly, like a tollbooth operator deciding whether to let a driver with no loose change pass through the gate. "Yeah," he said, "you straight then."

Randy leaned farther out his window. "Do you know where any dogs are?"

The driver laughed and slapped playfully at the steering wheel, and the man in the backseat grinned and shook his head. "Man, there's dogs everywhere around here." The automatic windows of the Oldsmobile slid closed. It rumbled on and disappeared after a low, wide turn around the next corner.

"They thought I was looking for drugs."

On the way back, the producer wanted to film the bus moving across the bridge with the St. Louis skyline and the Arch and the river in the background. With the wind rushing through his window, Randy turned up Tears for Fears. The Blazer pulled up alongside, with the camera lens resting on the open window.

"Look," Randy said, "I'm being filmed *and* driving across a bridge, and I'm not freaking out."

After Animal Planet aired the *Wild Rescues* segment about Randy, donations poured in from across the country. Randy sold his grooming shop to become the full-time executive director of Stray

Rescue. He won E-Town Radio's humanitarian award, he appeared on the Weather Channel explaining how to keep dogs safe in bad weather, and he advised the St. Louis public schools' preveterinary program.

With the help of Mindy Bier, he soon began writing a proposal for Maddie's Fund, which made multimillion-dollar grants to cities that attempt to make their shelters "no kill." The money would be used to lower euthanasia rates over a five-year period, through educational programs, shelter expansion, and massive spay-neuter campaigns in low-income areas.

In order to qualify for the grant, applicants must show that all the shelters in the designated city are willing to cooperate. In St. Louis, every shelter, including the city's animal-control agency, agreed—except the Humane Society of Missouri. HSM, the fourth-wealthiest Humane Society shelter in the country, refused to return Stray Rescue's letters and calls. With its $55 million endowment, Randy said, the HSM board of directors probably felt it didn't have to.

In early 2001, as Stray Rescue and its new collaborative of shelters tried to persuade HSM to join the grant proposal, tragedy struck St. Louis.

On the afternoon of March 4, a ten-year-old boy named Rodney McAllister crossed the street from his home to play basketball in Ivory Perry Park. Rodney's mother, battling drug addiction, had recently moved to St. Louis from southern Missouri to seek medical help. Because she had no phone, she regularly told her son to stay at friends' houses if he was out past dark, so when he didn't return home that night, she assumed he'd done just that.

Early the next morning, a man crossing the park found Rodney's mutilated body. He'd been attacked by a pack of stray dogs; several still hovered near the body. Rodney's basketball lay under a nearby tree.

As the St. Louis police chief, Ron Henderson, told the *St. Louis*

Post-Dispatch: "They were feeding off this kid. I've seen over 1,500 bodies, but I've never, never seen anything like this. Nobody has. . . . The pathologist said the kid was alive throughout the ordeal. . . . He suffered big time. I'll never forget it, I'll tell you that."

Horror settled over the city. Neighbors of the McAllister family told the media that stray dogs had roamed the streets in their area for years; but the dogs kept moving, and some were feral, so animal control workers—who had seen their agency's budget cut again and again over the years—never caught them.

The *Post-Dispatch* ran an editorial cartoon in which a circle of large, crazed dogs moved in on a tiny, terrified child. The drooling dogs were labeled "Drugs," "Gangs," "Failing Schools," "Abuse," "Poverty," "Lead Poisoning," and "Crime." The boy's T-shirt read "City Kids."

Civic leaders promised to work harder to catch stray dogs; they funneled emergency funds to the city's health department, which governs animal control. Within days, nine strays from Rodney's neighborhood were picked up and sent to the pound, and across the city, animal control wardens worked overtime to seize hundreds more.

News crews filmed the massive roundup. They filmed dogs chased through alleys, dogs chased through fields, dogs chased down the middle of streets with police officers and animal-control wardens close behind.

Every night, St. Louis watched dogs hauled out of empty buildings and dragged across the screen at the ends of snares. They saw wild puppies plucked out of junkyards while their half-wild mothers were wrestled to the ground. They watched frothing, shaking, starving dogs pulled from parks and empty cars and railroad yards and then watched them carried to the waiting city trucks and then watched the trucks carry their cargo off to the pound.

Television viewers saw the inside of the city shelters. The sterile cages. The terrified faces of dog after dog after dog. The door to the room where in the coming months the dogs were euthanized one after the other.

At a memorial service held for Rodney one week after his death, then-mayor Clarence Harmon asked the crowd of mourners: "Could we have done more?"

"Yes," Randy said at a town hall meeting, which Stray Rescue— along with Congressman William Lacy Clay, the West End Community Conference, and St. Louis alderman Irving Clay—sponsored one month later. "But killing stray dogs by the hundreds isn't the answer. We have to stop it before it's a problem."

The shelter collaborative's application for the Maddie's Fund grant now made headlines, and the HSM's refusal to sign on became the focus of the stories. HSM officials claimed that St. Louis "wasn't ready" for such a huge undertaking. Even after Randy lobbied the St. Louis board of aldermen and succeeded in getting a resolution passed that voiced the city's support of the application, HSM wouldn't budge.

"They just don't get it," Randy said one afternoon. "It's like any social issue. We have to be proactive. We have to be progressive. We can't just sit on our hands and wait for miracles to fall from the sky."

Late in 2002, HSM still hadn't signed on.

After the Animal Planet filming, Randy was also offered an administrative job with Pets Unlimited, one of the largest no-kill shelters in San Francisco. The organization would offer him a large salary (large by not-for-profit standards) to set up a stray-rescue program and would throw in moving expenses and find him a house on the beach as incentives. But he turned the job down.

"I don't know," he said one morning as he drove along Chouteau looking for Taz and Compton. "I'm not done here yet, I guess."

A new pack had moved into the warehouse, but the property was sold to a trucking company, which boarded up the warehouse and parked dozens of semis in the yard. The new pack—along with Lester—moved out for good. Randy saw Lester occasionally on the streets, but the old man, lost in delirium, seemed to have forgotten who he was.

"I wish I had done more to help him," Randy said. "I give him money whenever I see him, but . . . I don't know. He's trapped. They're all trapped, the dogs, the people who live in poverty, the people who can't deal with reality anymore. It's like they need so much help from the rest of us, only the rest of us aren't all willing to help."

In the coming months, the bus's engine gave out, and Randy bought a new van—a monstrous black Aztec with a CD player and air-conditioning in the back for the dogs. The bus stood in his drive way, a storage space for donated dog food.

But on the day of the Animal Planet taping, the bus was still clunking along. On the bridge from the East Side, with Tears for Fears in the tape deck and the wind roaring through the windows, as he passed the Arch and the riverboats and the St. Louis skyline, Randy turned toward the camera that pointed out at him from the Blazer. He smiled, and he flashed it a peace sign.

Randy and Hannah

Randy and Spanky, one of Bonnie's grown pups

J. B.

Sunny today

Bashful today

Sunshine today

J. B.

J. B.

To be a stray dog in most major cities is to be a dead dog walking. To be a stray is a death sentence, because there are few well-funded organizations that address the problem, so there is little hope for dogs stuck in the cycle of chaotic torture. What can one person do—especially one haunted by his own problems?

I can tell you with absolute certainty that I wasn't born to rescue dogs. I am no saint or hero. If I was, well, I would be a priest or a soldier, and this would be a completely different book. Growing up, I had more than my share of problems. I had a father who was abusive and a mother who was loyal and loving. Abusive; loyal and loving: no wonder I am a strange somebody. When I was a child, helping animals became a need; it was my crutch, my way with dealing with pain. Saving a cat or a dog saved a part of myself.

Living in fear as a child carried over into adulthood. As each year passed, I found myself, more and more, staying away from people, shying away from the mall, avoiding any place where people gathered. In the meantime, I kept helping animals.

When my dad died, I cried. What made his death especially punishing was that I was crying in relief. Now, I thought, I could go out and be this great, outgoing, interesting guy. Funny how life makes sure nothing is that easy. Mental note: Make a shrink appointment and rescue a stray dog.

The dogs I started rescuing were not cutesy-wootsy types, but dogs born on the city streets, those dying from abuse and starvation, those dying because they had been born. Almost everyone I knew discouraged me, and at times I felt like a leper without a colony to support me. They told me to "get a life." I had a life, just not the one they hoped for.

Sitting one day on the couch with Paul, I tried to explain why I do what I do. I told him about Hobo, a dog who lived by the train tracks and became my distant friend. Every day I headed down to the tracks to feed this multicolored Shepherd mix, and many times I would find him sitting under a train car watching me with that look that said, "Can I trust this human?"

We continued this daily feeding ritual for months. Sometimes Hobo would sprint off in a mad dash to get away from me; other times he would come within four feet of me as I threw hot dogs in his direction. I would sit and talk with him, while he would do the doggy head-cock and study every movement I made. He understood me, and I understood him. We were both afraid of life, and when I looked into his tortured eyes, guess who I saw? I saw me.

Hobo was killed by a train. I guess that was inevitable. The pain I felt added to my passion that much more. And it does every time I see a stray dog.

The point, I guess, is this: I can look back on my life and see how all of the pieces of the puzzle fit together. I'm not perfect, but I know that if it wasn't for the dogs, I would have ended up a lost soul with a bleak life. No one requires an epiphany to follow whatever their passions might be. They just have to pay attention to all of the little pieces, to their own life puzzle, and make sure that what isn't missing is compassion.

Randy Grim

Appendix: Animal Organizations

This is by no means an exhaustive list. It does not, for instance, include information about state, local, or breed-specific organizations, but it will give interested readers a good start. The Web sites not only give full explanations of the groups' particular philosophies, but they often provide dozens of links to similar organizations.

National Humane Organizations

- The Animal Abuse Prevention Agency
  7071 Warner Ave. Ste. F #444
  Huntington Beach, CA 92547
  (310) 364-2030
  toaapa@hotmail.com

- Animal Rescue Foundation
  P.O. Box 30215
  Walnut Creek, CA 94598
  (800) 567-1ARF
  www.tlr-arf.org

- The American Humane Association
  63 Inverness Drive East
  Englewood, CO 80112-5117
  (800) 227-4645
  www.americanhumane.org

- The American Society for the Prevention of Cruelty to Animals
  424 E. 92nd St.
  New York, NY 10128
  (212) 876-7700
  www.aspca.org

- Best Friends Sanctuary
  5001 Angel Canyon Rd.
  Kanab, UT 84741-5001
  (453) 644-2001
  www.bestfriends.org

- The Doris Day Animal League
  227 Massachusetts Ave., NE
  Washington, DC 20002
  www.ddal.org

- Humane America Animal Foundation
  P.O. Box 7
  Redondo Beach, CA 90277
  (310) 263-2930
  info@humaneamerica.org
  www.humaneamerica.org

- The Humane Society of the United States
  2100 L St., NW
  Washington, DC 20037
  www.hsus.org

- Maddie's Fund
  2223 Santa Clara Ave.
  Alameda, CA 94501-4416
  (510) 337-8989
  www.maddies.org

- The National Humane Education Society
  521-A East Market St.
  Leesburg, VA 20176
  (703) 777-8391
  nhesinformation@nhes.org
  www.nhes.org

- The Progressive Animal Welfare Society
  (425) 787-2500
  www.paws.org

Web Sites

- Stray Rescue of St. Louis
  www.strayrescue.org

- Adoption resources
  www.dogsneedingpeopleneedingdogs.org

- Directories of national and international humane societies, humane shelters, and rescue organizations
  United Animal Nations & Emergency Animal Rescue Service
  www.uan.org
  Hugs for Homeless Animals
  www.h4ha.org
  World Animal Net Directory
  www.worldanimal.net

The ShelterDogz Index

www.cardogz.com

Pet Finder USA

www.petfinder.org

Einstein's Online Pet Rescue Group

www.petrescue.com

PetShelter Network

www.petshelter.org

National Listing of Online Resources

www.creatures.com

Missing Pet Network

www.missingpet.net

- Directory of no-kill shelters
  Save Our Strays

  www.saveourstrays.com

- Animal rights
  In Defense of Animals

  www.idausa.org

  Alliance for Animal Rights

  www.envirolink.org/orgs/fcg/aar

  Animal Legal Defense Fund

  www.aldf.org

  Animal Protection Institute

  www.api4animals.org

  Animal Rights.Net

  www.animalrights.net

  The Fund for Animals

  www.fund.org

  Society for Animal Protective Legislation

  www.saplonline.org

Works Cited

Chapter Two

American Society for the Protection of Cruelty to Animals. Survey of pit bulls brought to shelters in 1999.

The American Veterinary Medical Association, "Dog Bite Prevention Message Points." 2001 (www.avma.org).

Apperson, J. "Board Sets Conditions for Return of Fighting Pit Bulls to Owners." *The Baltimore Sun*, 23 June 1999.

Associated Press. "Detroit Fights to Control Feral Dogs." Detroit, 15 May 1998.

Bahrampour, T. "New York Dogs." *The New York Times,* 12 Nov. 2000.

Baker, K. C. "To Fear or Not Fear Pit Bulls." *Daily News* (New York), 27 Feb. 1999.

Beck, A., and Rubin, H. "Ecological Behavior of Free-Ranging Urban Pet Dogs." *Applied Animal Ethology*, 8:161–168 (1980).

Brestrup, Craig. *Disposable Animals: Ending the Tragedy of Throwaway Pets.* Leander, TX.: Camino Bay Books, 1997.

Blankstein, A. "Student Attacked by Pack of Stray Dogs." *Los Angeles Times*, 4 Nov. 1999.

Boulard, G. "Louisiana City Is Going to the Dogs—Literally." *Los Angeles Times,* 27 Nov. 1991.

CNN. "Stray Animals, Abandoned Pets Overrunning America's Cities." Detroit, 30 Jan. 1997.

Esparza, S. "Detroit Battles Stray Dogs: Packs of Canines Roam Streets, Threatening Mail Carriers, Children." *The Detroit News*, 13 May 1998.

Hart, R. "It's the Law: Keep Dogs on Leashes." *Denver Post*, 5 Aug. 1999.

Hughes, J. "Deserted by Owners, Old Pets Become Pests." Associated Press, 4 Feb. 1997.

Humane Society of the United States. "HSUS Pet Overpopulation Estimates." 2000 (www.hsus.org).

Louv, R. "World Going to the Big, Mean Dogs." *San Diego Union-Tribune*, 18 June 2000.

Pfankuch, T. "Bad Owners Are Turning Pets into Problems." *Jacksonville Florida Times-Union*, 13 Apr. 2000.

Rivera, C. "With County's Stray Dog Population Soaring to 45,000, Authorities Are Fighting Public Health Threat." *Los Angeles Times*, 14 Nov. 1999.

Rodgers, T. "Oceanside Dogged by Stray Canines Near River." *San Diego Union-Tribune*, 16 June 1990.

Silver, J. D. "Safety Measures Under Review." *Pittsburgh Post-Gazette*, 27 May 1998.

Strauss, J. "Attacks Lead to Hunt for Packs of Wild Dogs." *Indianapolis Star*, 5 Dec. 1998.

Sullivan, D. "Police Shooting More Dogs Used by Drug Dealers." *Daily News of Los Angeles*, 20 July 1999.

Wilson, G. "Dogs Loose in Zoo May be Shot." *Daily News* (New York), 11 Jan. 2001.

Chapter Three

Cohn, J. "How Wild Wolves Became Domestic Dogs." *BioScience* 47:725–30 (1997).

Fox, M. W. *The Dog: Its Domestication and Behavior*. New York: Garland STPM Press, 1978.

Mech, L. D. "Alpha Status, Dominance, and Division of Labor in Wolf Packs." *Canadian Journal of Zoology* 77:1196–1203 (1999).

———. "The Wolf: The Ecology and Behavior of an Endangered Species." Minneapolis: University of Minnesota Press, 1970.

Morell, V. "The Origins of Dogs: Running with the Wolves." *Science* 276:1647–48 (1997).

Morey, D. F. "The Evolution of the Domestic Dog." *American Scientist* 82:336–47 (1994).

Nova #2415. "Wild Wolves." Broadcast Transcript, 11 Nov. 1997.

Pet Behavior Clinic. "Leadership/Alpha." 1995 (www.pethelp.net).

Scott, J. P., and Fuller, J. L. *Genetics and the Social Behavior of the Dog*. Chicago: University of Chicago Press (1965).

Weidensaul, S. "Tracking America's First Dog: Carolina Dogs." *Smithsonian* 29:44–52 (1999).

Wayne, R. K. "Molecular Evolution of the Dog Family." *Trends in Genetics* 9:218–25 (1993).

Chapter Five

American Game Dog Times Online. (www.agdt.com).

Apperson, J. "Board Sets Conditions for Return of Fighting Pit Bulls to Owners." *The Baltimore Sun*, 23 June 1999.

Associated Press. "Authorities Bust Dog-Fighting Ring." *Commercial Appeal* (Memphis), 13 Aug. 2000.

———. "Judge's Bite Worse Than Bark for Cruel Dog Owner." *Commercial Appeal* (Memphis), 30 Oct. 1999.

Bahrampour, T. "Neighborhood Report: New York Dogs." *The New York Times*, 12 Nov. 2000.

"Boudreaux' Eli: Vintage Match Report." *American Pit Bull Reporter Magazine*, 2000 (www.pitbulls.com).

Buser, L. "Memphis Animal Control Confiscates 50 Pit Bulls." *Tennessean*, 1 Aug. 1999.

Chicago Department of Animal Control. "Animal Fighting: Inhumane and Illegal." (www.ci.chi.us).

Conley, C. "Six Arrested, 21 Pit Bulls Seized at Homes." *Commercial Appeal* (Memphis), 21 July 1999.

Deadman Kennels. "Welcome to My Yard." 1997 (www.delanet.com/~badboyz/deadman.htm).

Garret, C. "Cops Crack Down on Dog Fighting." *The Detroit News*, 12 Apr. 2000.

Humane Society of the United States. "Animal Fighting." 1998 (www.hsus.org).

"Is Dog Fighting Cruel?" Suzi and Dowser's House: A Boxer and Pit Bull Page. 1997 (www.geocites.com/Heartland/Hills/4805/is_cruel.htm).

Jones, Y. "Dog Fights Lead to Seizure of 12 Animals From Memphis Home." *Commercial Appeal* (Memphis), 1 Dec. 1999.

Krause, K., and Melendez, M. "Regional Task Force Sought to Muzzle Dog Fights." *Sun-Sentinel* (Fort Lauderdale), 15 July 2000.

Michigan Humane Society. "Michigan Humane Society Cruelty Investigators Rescue 21 Dogs From Fighting Ring." 1999 (www.detnews.com/mhs).

Othon, N. "Dog-Fighting Charges Filed Against Delray Man." *Sun-Sentinel* (Fort Lauderdale), 10 Sept. 2000.

"Pit Rules, with Cajun Variations." *Sporting Dog Online*. 2001 (www.sportingdog.com).

Raferty, C. "Pit Bulls a Dying Breed." *San Jose Mercury News*, 11 Jan. 2000.

Santiago, R. "The War Against Animal Fighting." *Daily News* (New York), 18 Feb. 2001.

Santich, K., and Bloodsworth, D. "Looking in the Pen of an Illegal Dog Fight." Associated Press, 3 Feb. 2001.

Steinberg, N., and Main, F. "Born to be Killers." *Chicago Sun-Times*, 5 Nov. 2000.

Stockman, F. "Man Fatally Stabs Pit Bull." *The Boston Globe*, 29 Aug. 2000.

Toledo Humane Society. "Dog Fighting: A Community Problem." 2001 (www.toledohumanesociety.com).

Zamichow, N. "Deliberate Quest for Ferocity Bred Dog that Killed Woman." *Los Angeles Times*, 1 Feb. 2001.

Chapter Six

Cohn, J. "How Wild Wolves Became Domestic Dogs." *BioScience* 47:725–30 (1997).

Coppinger, R. "Why Dogs Bark." *Smithsonian* vol. 21, no. 10, pp. 119–28. Jan. 1991.

Coren, S. *The Intelligence of Dogs*. New York: Bantam, 1994.

Fox, M. W. *The Dog: Its Domestication and Behavior*. New York: Garland STPM Press, 1978.

Morey, D. F. "The Early Evolution of the Domestic Dog." *American Scientist* 82:336–47 (1994).

Scott, J. P., and Fuller, J. L. *Genetics and the Social Behavior of the Dog*. Chicago: University of Chicago Press, 1965.

Chapter Seven
Beck, A. "Ecology of Unwanted and Uncontrolled Pets." Proceedings of the National Conference on the Ecology of the Surplus Dog and Cat Problem, 1974.
Brooks, C. "Mange." Veterinary Information Network, Inc., 2001 (www.vin.com).
Bullock, J. "Demodectic Mange." Bark Bytes, Inc., 1998 (www.barkbytes.com).
Centers for Disease Control. "Human Rabies Prevention—United States, 1999 Recommendations of the Advisory Committee on Immunization Practices." (www.cdc.gov).
———. "Rabies: Epidemiology." 2001 (www.cdc.com).
Coblentz, B. "Street Life Takes a Toll on Animals." *Veterinary Medical News*. Mississippi State University, 1997.
Hutton, K. "Zoonotic Diseases." *Dog Owner's Guide*. Cincinnati, Oh.: Canis Major Publications, 2001.
Krebs, J. W.; Smith, J.; Rupprecht, C.; Childs, J. "Rabies Surveillance in the United States." vol. 11, no. 12 (1997) p. 217.
National Institute of Allergy and Infectious Diseases Rabies Fact Sheet (2000).
Woolf, N. "Canine Worms." *Dog Owner's Guide*. Cincinnati, Ohio: Canis Major Publications, 2001.

Chapter Eight
American Humane Association. "Legislation." 2001 (vww.americanhumane.org).
American Kennel Club. "Canine Legislation Position Statements." 2001 (www.akc.org).
Animal People Online "Editorial: Self Defeat in Los Angeles." May 2000 (www.animalpeopleonline.org).
Betsch, Michael. "Activist Group Urges Civil Rights for Pets." CNS News. 31 July 2001(www.cnsnews.com).
Cleek, Margaret. "Instead of Breeding Bans." *Animal People News*. 1993 (www.animalpeoplenews.org).
Fox, M.; Beck, A.; and Blackman, E. "Behavior and Ecology of a Small Group of Urban Dogs." *Applied Animal Ethology* 1:119–37 (1975).
Humane Society of the United States. "Government Affairs: State Legislation." 2001 (www.hsus.org).
In Defense of Animals. "Relating to Our Dogs: Are We Owners or Guardians?" *Dog Watch Newsletters*, July 2001.
Katz, Elliot. "We Are Guardians: People Who Adopt Animals Need Recognition for Acting Ethnically." *San Francisco Chronicle*, 2 Sept. 1999.
Office of Illinois State Representative Sara Feigenholtz. "House Approves 'Pet Friendly' License Plate Bill." Press release, 22 Feb. 2001.
Pringle, Paul. "Toughest Dog Law's Fines Stiff for Canines Not Spayed." *Dallas Morning News*, 14 May 2000.
Rosen, Ambuja. "Dogs in Chains: If We Stop Calling Dogs Our Property, Will They Become More Liberated?" *Dogs Today*, Aug. 2000.
State of Rhode Island. "An Act Relating to Animals and Animal Husbandry." HOI-6119 Introduced to the General Assembly by Reps. Cicilline Dennigan and W. J. Murphy on 28 Feb. 2001.

Woolf, Norma. National Animal Interest Alliance. "Is it compassionate to cut back on dog breeding?" (*www.naiaonline.org*).

Chapter Nine
Budiansky, S. *The Truth About Dogs.* New York: Penguin, 2000.
Coren, S. *The Intelligence of Dogs.* New York: Free Press, 1994.
———. *How to Speak Dog.* New York: Simon & Schuster, 2000.
Fogle, B. *The Dog's Mind.* New York: Macmillan, 1990.
Mech, D. "Alpha Status, Dominance, and Division of Labor in Wolf Packs." *Canadian Journal of Zoology* 77:1196–1203 (1999).
Milani, M. *The Body Language and Emotion of Dogs.* New York: William Morrow, 1986.
Schmidt, P., and Mech, D. "Wolf Pack Size and Food Acquisition." *American Naturalist* 150 (4): 513–17 (1997).
Scott, P., and Fuller, J. *Genetics and Social Behavior of the Dog.* Chicago: University of Chicago Press, 1965.

Chapter Ten
Ecenbarger, W. "Scandal of America's Puppy Mills." *Readers Digest,* Feb. 1999, pp. 118–23.
Humane Society of the United States. "Puppy Mill Facts." 1999 (www.hsus.org).
In Defense of Animals. "Puppy Mills Campaign." 2001 (www.idausa.org).
Italiano, L. "Puppy Mill Scandal." *New York Post,* 20 Oct. 1996.
Office of Missouri State Auditor Claire McCaskill. "Audit of the Animal Care Facilities Inspection Program." Report No. 2001–09 (2001).
People for the Ethical Treatment of Animals. Letter to U.S. Department of Agriculture, 19 Aug. 1999 (www.helppuppies.com).
Sheeter, C. "Should Pet Stores Sell Puppies?" *ANS 420: Ethical Issues in Animal Agriculture.* Feb. 2000.
Smith, L. "Puppy Mill Nightmare." *Dog Owner's Guide.* Cincinnati, Ohio: Canis Major Publications 2001.
Stark, K. "Breeding Dogs." *Philadelphia Inquirer,* 1995.
Townsend, K. "No Puppy Mills." 1998. (*www.nopuppymills.com*).
U.S. Department of Agriculture. "The Animal Welfare Act." Animal and Plant Health Inspection Services." 1998.
WorldNow, WTNH, and Associated Press. "Backyard Breeders." New Haven/Hartford, Conn., 12 Nov. 1997.

Chapter Twelve
Adams, R. "Three Students Hospitalized After Pit Bulls Board Bus." *Republican-American* (Waterbury, Conn.), 13 Oct. 2000.
American Veterinary Medical Association. "Dog Bite Prevention Campaign: Nipping a Problem in the Bud." (www.avma.org).
Associated Press. "Three-Year-Old Killed by Pit Bull." 28 June 2000.
———. "Census Worker Dead: Pack of Dogs Found Feeding on 71-Year-Old Woman's Body." 12 June 2000.

Beck, A.; Loring, H.; and Lockwood, R. "The Ecology of Dog Bite Injury in St. Louis, Missouri." *Public Health Reports* 90:262–69 (1975).

Beck, A., and Jones, B. "Unreported Dog Bites in Children." *Public Health Reports* 100:315–21 (1985).

Centers for Disease Control. "Dog Bite Related Fatalities—United States, 1995–1996." *Morbidity and Mortality Weekly Report* 46:463–67 (1997).

"Child Mauled to Death by Dogs." *The Washington Post*, 6 Mar. 2001.

Derr, M. "It Takes Training and Genes to Make a Mean Dog Mean." *The New York Times*, 13 Feb. 2001.

Gershman, K.; Sacks, J.; and Wright, J. "Which Dogs Bite? A Case-Control Study of Risk Factors." *Pediatrics* 6:913–17 (1994).

Guido, M., and Foo, M. "Pit Bulls Attack, Wound Three in San Jose Apartment Complex." *San Jose Mercury News*, 10 Apr. 2001.

McClam, E. "Bad Dog: Report Says Rottweilers Involved in Most Fatal Attacks." Associated Press, 15 Sept. 2000.

Sacks, J.; Kresnow, M.; and Houston, B. "Dog Bites: How Big a Problem?" *Injury Prevention* 2:52–54 (1996).

Sacks, J., et al. "Breeds of Dogs Involved in Fatal Human Attacks in the United States Between 1979–1998." *Journal of the American Veterinary Medical Association* 217:836–40 (2000).

"San Francisco Officers Fire 30 Bullets to Kill Pit Bull." *San Francisco Chronicle*, 23 March 2002.

Scott, J., and Fuller, J. *Genetics and Social Behavior of the Dog.* Chicago: University of Chicago Press, 1965.

Serpell, J. *The Domestic Dog. Its Evolution, Behavior and Interactions with People.* New York: Cambridge University Press, 1995.

Wagenknecht, P. *A Report That Addresses Vicious Dog Attacks.* Apr. 2001.

Chapter Fifteen

Johnson, Greg. "Popular Boy's Quiet Side May Have Reflected Bleak Home Life." *St. Louis Post-Dispatch*, 8 March 2001.